It Came to Me on a Whim

Maria Bouroncle

It Came to Me on a Whim

The Story of Ingeborg Andersson,
Child Murderess

Translated from the Swedish by Tom Ellett

SAGA Egmont

It Came to Me on a Whim - The Story of Ingeborg Andersson, Child Murderess

Translated by Tom Ellett

Original title: *Det kom för mig i en hast - Historien om barnamörderskan Ingeborg Andersson*

Original language: Swedish
Cover image: Shutterstock
Copyright © 2018, 2022 Maria Bouroncle and SAGA Egmont

All rights reserved

ISBN: 9788728446096

1. POD edition

No part of this publication may be reproduced, stored in a retrievial system, or transmitted, in any form or by any means without the prior written permission of the publisher, nor, be otherwise circulated in any form of binding or cover other than in which it is published and without a similar condition being imposed on the subsequent purchaser.

www.sagaegmont.com
Saga is a subsidiary of Egmont. Egmont is Denmark's largest media company and fully owned by the Egmont Foundation, which donates almost 13,4 million euros annually to children in difficult circumstances.

For Tor, Efraim and Lucia

To the Reader

The parts of the text in italics are translated transcripts of actual letters, historical records and other documents.

The text in regular type is a fictionalized reimagining of these scenes, but the main characters and the locations are real.

Farewell

We request
the honour of your company
at the funeral of our dearly loved children
Tor Ingvar
Anders Artur Efraim
Inga Britta Lucia
at Vesene Parish Church
on Easter Monday, 1929, at 5 p.m.

Ingeborg and Artur Andersson

Visitation at the home of the bereaved, Haggården, from 2:30 p.m.

The four well-groomed schoolboys in black suits bore a heavy burden. The small, white-painted open coffin contained Efraim, their friend and neighbour. Efraim, a little boy named after his grandfather. Efraim, a little boy who was only three years old. He looked as though he was sleeping, lying there on his back in his white nightshirt. His hands were folded across his chest, resting on the blanket woven by his mother, clutching a white rose.

At an unnaturally slow pace, the boys made their way up the aisle of the packed village church of a community in mourning. Overcome by the solemnity of their task, the heavy responsibility etched on their faces, they were barely able to lift their feet. Silently, inwardly, they counted down the number of steps to the chancel. They needed something constant to hold on to.

> So I, when Sin
> And Hell begin
> To threaten my Undoing,
> Run to the side
> Of Christ, and hide
> Me from the threaten'd Ruin.[1]

The congregation sang a hymn. But what good was singing when it failed to dispel the sorrow?

The verger, a practical man who knew how to foster a sense of security out here in the backwoods, had placed juniper sprigs in each pew to ward off evil. The scent of the bushes soothed the congregation, who were unsure of how to behave on an occasion like this, of how to console a devastated family.

Time heals everything, people say.

They were not saying that today. Time does not heal everything. Not the incomprehensible. Empty, uncomprehending eyes stared straight ahead. The resin in the spruce logs crackled in the fireplace, but the heat failed to warm the hundred frozen souls, or to drive the moisture from their wet coats. Steam rose toward the windows, causing them to fog up. The boys counted the juniper sprigs.

A solitary, faltering man followed the boys. Until last week, he had been the object of much envy in the village. At the age of thirty-six, Artur seemed to have it all: a pretty young wife, three healthy children and a large farm. Now, he was a prematurely old man, bent under the weight of the second coffin on his right shoulder. The coffin of his eldest son, Tor. Five-year-old Tor, who was supposed to inherit the farm and follow in his father's footsteps.

Artur's brother carried the third coffin. It contained Lucia, the youngest child, whom no-one had yet got to know properly. Now she was lying on her side, ensconced in the bedlinen that would have been given to her on her wedding day. She was sucking her thumb, just as she used to when her father put her to bed at night.

The little procession stopped in front of the altar. A heavy silence descended within the solid granite walls as the last notes of the funeral march faded away. The men and the boys set down the draped coffins in front of three small wreaths of shiny green leaves with white flowers and ribbons. They lit the candles in the five-arm candelabra on the pedestal. The sulfurous smell of the matches mixed with the heavy scent of Easter lilies.

The two young men honoured with the task of carrying the ceremonial mourning staffs assumed their positions on each side of the coffins. A flimsy black veil fluttered from the crucifix atop each staff. The pastor scattered the petals of a white rose over the three siblings in their beds and read from Johan Olof Wallin's poem *Angel of Death*:

> They go so peaceful in God to slumber,
> They greet so joyful the final day:
> No tribulations their rest encumber,
> No visitations of fortune's sway.
> No longer thwarted,
> As earth compels us,
> They have departed,
> The spirit tells us,
> And their achievements shall follow them.[2]

Artur produced a photograph from the inside pocket of his jacket: a well-thumbed confirmation card showing a lanky girl around the age of fifteen. She was wearing a long black skirt and a long-sleeved black blouse with a white ruffle. The bobbin lace was secured by a pin under her chin. The girl had a serious expression. Artur discreetly slid the photograph of Ingeborg under the blanket in Lucia's coffin.

"She didn't mean it," he whispered. "She didn't know what she was doing."

Artur took his seat on the right-hand side of the aisle, next to his mother in the pew reserved for the family. Ingeborg — who didn't know what she was doing — was not present.

No. 119
VÄNERSBORG PENITENTIARY
*When corresponding with the sender of this letter, the envelope must be addressed as shown above: inmate number (**not** name) and the name and postal address of the correctional institution. However, the letter inside must bear both the inmate's number and his full name.*
Letters to inmates should be written in ink, in legible handwriting, and must contain only messages concerning personal matters. Press clippings and the like must not be enclosed. Paper, envelopes, stamps and soap are obtainable from the institution and must not be sent to inmates.
Form No. 4008
Board of Corrections, Stockholm, 1926

Sunday

My dear Artur

Its so nice I am feeling a bit beter here and everyone is so kind and nice I think and I get to go out every day which is so nice and I can knit socks and stop and read I also have a hymbook and other books as well the doctor comes to see me sometime the Chaplin came to see me it was so nice he said I will be forgiven for what I done which I am very sorry for I think about the children all the time and about you but forgive me I didnt know what I was doing O God if it could be undone. are Farmor and Holger Elsa very sad what did father and mother say is father sick

    I am eating better now I get soup peas and meat potatoes and herring fish and other things which is so good, poridge milk and fresh bread And then I get coffee and pastrys every day you cant imagin how good and we never drank such good coffee at home just imagin if I didnt get it

    just imagin if I could get well again. I feel so tired when I have been outside now I am sleeping better to begin with I slept so bad, but I can never forget the children and you.

    And we have a church service every Sunday that is so grand it is just like being in our church. it would be nice if you could come here but if you cant come please write, now I cant write any more so lots of love to you all, give my love to Father and mother and comfort them, love to Tali

I think I am in a convalesent home it is so hard to think about the children I dont understand why I done it. they were so sweet and inocent those little children. why did I do that. come soon it would be so nice to see you again. now I have had dinner potatoes meat soup,

Ingeborg

The Washtub

Two withered geraniums stood in the window. Bright red petals had fallen to the windowsill, dried out and shrivelled up, turning a darker, blood-red shade. Ingeborg, who was still not dressed, was sitting at the kitchen table with her head in her hands, gazing out at the steadily melting snow. Water trickled down the branches and dripped to the ground, perforating the crust on the snow.

"Aren't you going to finish your porridge?" inquired Artur, Ingeborg's husband, looking up from his newspaper.

He was sitting across from her, reading an article about a Swedish expert committee that was drawing up proposals on sterilization. On receiving no answer, he got up, cleared the table and called for his son, Tor.

"Help your mother with the dishes. She's got a lot to do today."

Artur was the president of the local rifle club and had invited its members to his home tomorrow for their first meeting of the year. He had asked Ingeborg to bake some wheat loaves for them to have with their coffee, and to tidy up indoors while he and his brother went out into the forest to chop wood. Piles of dirty laundry were strewn across the bedroom floor, and he had no clean trousers to wear.

"Shall I bring the washtub in, so you don't have to stand out there in the freezing cold washhouse to do the laundry?" he asked his wife, but the only response came from Tor who, young though he was, nodded on his mother's behalf from the sink.

Artur pulled on his boots and walked across the yard. The sun was out and, as it thawed, the frozen gravel resembled a grimy, viscous gruel. As he opened the washhouse door, the acrid smell of newly skinned fox hit him. Artur had landed a direct hit the previous week, having put out bait and lain in wait for several nights running. From the hide on the hill, he had spied the red fox stealing down to the meadows. The animal had fallen to the ground as soon as he opened fire. Artur stepped inside and stroked the soft fur hanging by the mouth from a hook in the ceiling.

This will make a fine boa for Ingeborg, he thought, wishing he could give her a full fur coat — although that would probably give the other village women a heart attack.

Artur has delusions of grandeur, the locals would say.

Making haste, he carried the large copper washtub into the kitchen and filled it with hot water from the tank and the pans on the stove. It was nearly half past nine.

"Do you need a hand with anything else before I go?" he asked, walking toward the kitchen door.

The floorboards creaked. His question unanswered, Artur turned to his wife and went on:

"Maybe it wasn't such a good idea to attempt all this lot in a single day. Do you think you can manage to have dinner ready by half past twelve?"

Artur opened the door and lingered in the hall. He opened his mouth and closed it again.

"Look after yourself and the children," he mumbled, and left without receiving any answer.

"Are you really going to take Blaze out in this weather?" asked Artur's mother, who was known to the family as Farmor, when he knocked on the door of the cottage to collect his brother and the farmhand.

"He can manage to haul some firewood, the old nag. It's not even a half-day's work. I can't let the children freeze, can I?" replied Artur.

"No, of course not. But don't overdo it, like you did last summer when the plough broke. You foolishly let the horse rest while you carried the machinery into the village for repair," said Farmor, patting her eldest son on the shoulder. "By the way, can I borrow a sieve?"

"There's one at home, in the wooden bin in the pantry. Tor can run over with it after dinner. Ingeborg has promised to have it ready by half past twelve."

"It's good that she's starting to feel better," said Farmor.

Ingeborg rose slowly from the kitchen chair. She took out the washboard and assumed her position on a wooden stool next to the large tub. As she was about to start scrubbing Artur's foul-smelling work trousers, her mind wandered and she sat there with the partially wet dungarees in her lap. Her nightgown became wetter and wetter, and the drops of water formed a puddle on the floor. The cat mewed and rubbed its black coat around Ingeborg's legs.

"What are you thinking about, Mama?" asked Tor.

The hands of the American clock advanced haltingly across the elegant clock face with its Roman numerals, as the water in the washtub grew colder by the minute. Every half-hour, the striking of the clock resonated through the silent kitchen. Ten o'clock. Half past ten. Eleven. Artur had bought the clock for his wife at an auction last summer. He had searched long and hard to find one with hand-painted violets on its glass door.

"I've left my watch at home, damn it!" said Artur to his brother. "I'm going back to get it. So I'll take the first load to the woodshed while I'm at it."

Half an hour later, Artur had unloaded the logs from the sledge and was walking quickly across the yard toward the house. He scaled the back steps in two bounds and stamped the slush off his feet on the spruce twigs outside the door. He struggled out of his rubber boots on a blue-striped rag rug in the hall, leaving a lone sock made from leftover yarn stranded on the wooden floor. He opened the door and popped his head in.

"Damn it, it's cold out there!" exclaimed Artur, clasping his arms around him. "Why haven't you opened the blind in the bedroom?"

Ingeborg was sitting at the kitchen table, fiddling with the watch Artur had left behind on the wax tablecloth with its green floral pattern.

"We got all the way out into the woods before I noticed I'd forgotten my watch. What time is it anyway?" asked Artur.

"See for yourself," replied Ingeborg slowly.

Artur glanced at the American clock on its shelf in the corner. Half past eleven. So they would have time to fetch another load from the woods before dinner. But first, he would just go and open the blind — it shouldn't be left down in broad daylight. What would the neighbours say? He walked across the kitchen in the direction of the bedroom. The lug of the copper washtub was sticking out from behind the half-open door. But Artur had left the washtub in the kitchen. Why had Ingeborg dragged it in there? She should have finished the laundry ages ago, anyway. Suddenly it struck him: the windows had not fogged up as they usually did in the winter when she hung up the laundry indoors. There was a sour smell, and the house was unusually quiet.

"Where are the children?" he asked, receiving no answer.

On opening the door to the bedroom, Artur saw the large, round copper washtub sitting just inside. It was half full of water, and the rest had spilled out onto the floor. The water left in the tub contained traces of vomit. Tor was on his knees on the floor, his thick hair wet through. Efraim and Lucia were hanging over the right-hand side of the tub. Efraim's head was submerged, and Artur fell to his knees and pulled him out, trying to shake his beloved child back to life. Efraim's head and the clothes at his neck were wet, and there was a trickle of blood from his left ear. The boy's body had already started to grow cold, so Artur grabbed a wool blanket and wrapped it around him. It could not end like this. Efraim's life could not end like this.

"Ingeborg, help me!" yelled Artur.

His forearm brushed against Lucia's cheek, which was warm. He let go of Efraim, and the boy dropped to the floor with a thud. Clasping the girl to his chest, Artur thumped her hard on the back several times, praying to God that she would come to with a cough and throw up on his shoulder. He wished so fervently for her to start breathing that he could almost feel her chest moving. But nothing happened.

"What are we going to do, Mother?" whispered Artur when the children's grandmother and aunt turned up a little while later to pick up the sieve.

"What's happened?" cried Farmor, rushing into the bedroom, where she fell to her knees.

Artur was sitting in a puddle on the floor, surrounded by his two sons, slowly rocking Lucia back and forth in his arms. Farmor embraced her son from behind, looking at her dead grandchildren and wishing she could lift them out of this sorrow, bring them to safety. Artur's sister Elsa, who had been standing silently in the doorway, began hitting her sister-in-law and screaming hysterically.

"Get out, you're crazy!"

Then she collapsed on the floor in tears.

"Dear children. My dear children. What are we going to do?" whispered Farmor quietly to herself, stroking their cold, wet limbs.

"I won't survive this, Mother," whispered Artur.

This is my fault, thought Farmor.

She stood up wearily and lifted Tor onto the bed. He had grown so tall, but was slight like his mother. Efraim, although a year younger, was already heavier. She gently removed the wet shirts from the boys, caressing Tor's cheek and stroking a few stray hairs out of Efraim's face. She placed them side by side in the bed and tucked them in. Her beautiful grandchildren. Lastly, she tried to release Lucia from her son's clasp, but Artur refused to let go, burying his face in the girl's little body. Aged only fifteen months, she had still not grown into a little person in her own right. Tor was always carrying her around.

You're spoiling her, Farmor used to say.

More fool me, she thought. Now, she wished she had carried all three of them all the time. Carried them through life.

"Yes, what are we going to do?" she said, stroking her son's hair.

Artur looked up, staring straight ahead with unseeing eyes. Farmor picked up the little girl, placed her in the bed between her two brothers, and closed her eyes. Lying there on the soft white pillows, the children looked as though they were sleeping. On the pillowcases were two delicately embroidered initials: I for Ingeborg and A for Artur. Ingeborg had brought the pillowcases in her bridal chest.

Farmor walked toward the kitchen and stopped in front of the telephone on the wall. Ingeborg was still sitting in silence at the kitchen table, clasping the watch. It was one o'clock. Farmor placed her hand on the heavy metal telephone, turned the wooden crank several times, and picked up the receiver.

"Could you put me through to the sheriff's office, please?" she said to the operator at the Siene Kyrkby exchange.

The Sheriff

"Saddle the horse! We must get to Vesene right away!"

As he hung up the telephone, Sheriff Dahlstrand was sitting at his desk across from the cells, looking out of the barred window of the Gäsene courthouse. He was not sure he had understood everything Farmor had told him, despite asking her to repeat herself several times. The line was bad and she had stumbled over her words.

"You must come with me as a witness."

The clerk went out to hook up the horse and wagon. The sheriff put on his doublebreasted uniform of blue cloth with gold-plated buttons. The mare shook her mane and trod impatiently on the spot while the clerk fastened the sheriff's brown briefcase to the bed of the wagon with a couple of leather straps.

"We're all set," said the clerk, picking up the reins, after the two men had taken their seats.

The trusty steed set off down the hill at a trot. In the next village, an old man sawing logs watched inquisitively and waved. His wife was hanging out fish on a line by the river.

After little more than twenty minutes, they arrived. In the middle of the yard, an abandoned horse, harnessed to a sledge, was whinnying. A light brown hound, chained to a rope running from the barn to the outhouse, was trotting back and forth, barking. As the visitors alighted from their wagon, the dog slunk into his kennel to hide. The sheriff and the clerk approached the front door of the house and peered in through the glass. Having seen them arrive, Elsa opened the door and invited them in.

"Good afternoon," began the sheriff, taking off his coat. "So tell me, what has happened here?"

Wordlessly, Elsa took the sheriff's gold-braided cap, which bore the Älvsborg county coat of arms, and pointed toward the bedroom. The sheriff made his way through the hall while the clerk dried off his galoshes before following. A woman with silvery grey hair was sitting on the edge of the bed next to three children, crying quietly, her hand resting on one child's arm.

As he caught sight of the washtub and the sour smell hit him, the sheriff realized the children were dead.

"Oh my God!" he exclaimed, standing dumbstruck in the doorway holding a hand to his face.

"Sorry for your loss," he said once he had pulled himself together.

"Sorry for your loss," repeated the clerk mechanically, taking out a pen and writing the date, Friday, March 22, 1929, in his notebook.

"What has happened here?" asked the sheriff again, stepping into the room.

Artur was still sitting on the wet floor, his arms clasped around his knees, rocking back and forth. The sheriff placed a hand on his shoulder.

"My daughter and I came over to borrow a sieve," began Farmor, placing a hand over her mouth. "By then they had already passed away."

The clerk turned to a new page and began making notes. "Were they in the bed?"

"No, I put them to bed. They were so cold and wet."

The sheriff took out a measuring tape.

"One hundred and five centimetres tall, slight build, normal musculature," he mumbled, describing five-year-old Tor.

"Would you like a cup of coffee, sheriff?" asked Farmor, getting up.

"Please don't go to any trouble on our account," replied the sheriff, waving his hand dismissively.

"We were going to have one anyway."

Farmor went into the kitchen, where Ingeborg was still sitting quietly at the table, fiddling with Artur's watch. With trembling hands, Farmor took out the best china from the varnished sideboard in the parlour. She then had a look in the pantry, but managed to find only a few old, dry jitterbugs, a kind of puff pastry filled with meringue. These were Ingeborg's favourite cakes, but she had not baked any for a long time. Farmor considered popping home to fetch some wheat buns, but assumed the two gentlemen had just had dinner. At any rate, the clerk smelled of cooking.

"Four-year-old, well developed, normal build. Girl, fifteen months, normally developed for her age, normal build, unremarkable musculature," the sheriff dictated.

Farmor removed the coffee pan from the stove and gripped the countertop with both hands. Leaning forward, she took a deep breath before straightening up and returning to the bedroom. Standing in the doorway, without looking at the children, she managed to hold her emotions in check as she announced:

"The coffee is ready."

"Thank you, ma'am," replied the sheriff. Turning back to the clerk, he added, "No sign of external violence," before following Farmor into the kitchen.

The sheriff put the measuring tape in his pocket and sat down opposite Ingeborg.

"I'm afraid I have nothing to offer you with your coffee," said Farmor apologetically as she served the hot drink, the pan shaking in her hand.

"Thank you, ma'am, thank you very much. That will warm us up nicely in this cold weather."

Farmor drank her coffee at the stove. Elsa was standing by the dresser.

"Why did you do what you did?" inquired the sheriff, addressing Ingeborg.

There was no response. Ingeborg continued staring out of the window and fiddling with her husband's watch, passing it back and forth from one hand to the other. But she said nothing. She did not know how to answer the question. She did not know why she had done it. It was just a notion that came to her.

"Were they not good children?" the sheriff continued, after receiving no reply.

Yes, they were good children. They were never particularly troublesome or sickly. Tor had asthma, of course, but it had almost cleared up recently.

"Did you and your husband exchange any harsh words this morning?"

Artur and Ingeborg never exchanged any harsh words. Artur had helped the children get dressed before he set out for the woods. All that Ingeborg had to do was to feed them breakfast. What had happened to the oatmeal she got out? Did the porridge get burnt? The children could be so unruly when they were hungry.

"Did you and your husband exchange any harsh words today?" repeated the sheriff.

"No," replied Ingeborg.

"Can you tell me what happened, Ingeborg?"

"I took the eldest first," she said calmly but distantly.

"Why did you take the boy's life?" inquired the sheriff, receiving no answer.

He rephrased his question but it remained unanswered.

"Why did you do it?" he asked, trying for a third time.

"I don't know."

"Are you quite well?"

"I don't think I am insane."

Ingeborg had been feeling down at heart lately. Her appetite had disappeared and she had lost weight. She was sleeping badly and felt tired. Now, she didn't know how to answer all the sheriff's questions. She knew her surname was Andersson but couldn't tell him her first names or what year she was born. She knew she had several brothers and sisters but couldn't remember how many. Nor could she remember where she went to school or where she was confirmed. But she could remember the day Artur proposed.

"To what do we owe the honour of this visit?" Artur's mother had said. "You might have told me you were going to bring your fiancée home, so I could have the coffee ready!"

Ingeborg had quickly pulled away her hand, which Artur had been holding.

"You're scaring the life out of us, Mother!" Artur had said "I thought you'd gone into town with Elsa?"

"Your sister's piano lesson was cancelled. The teacher is off sick. There's a nasty bug going around. Good afternoon, Miss Ingeborg," Artur's mother had said after climbing the stairs to the upstairs hall.

"Good afternoon, ma'am," Ingeborg had replied, curtseying deeply with her gaze fixed on a twig in the floorboards.

"Call me Farmor, my dear," Artur's mother had said before returning to her cottage.

"The wife cannot be persuaded to talk coherently about what has happened, but answers most of my questions with a simple affirmative or negative." The sheriff summed up the interview and rose from the table.

"Right, well then," he said, pausing for a moment. "We must be on our way."

Farmor hurried out of the kitchen, before returning with a soft, round hat, which she attached to Ingeborg's head with a couple of hairpins. She tried repeatedly to tuck in Ingeborg's short hair, which was sticking out below the brown brim, but it would not stay put. Farmor disappeared again, returning this time with a scarf, which she wrapped around Ingeborg's head.

"There we are! Now the hat won't blow off along the way," she said.

"I must ask you to come with me, Ingeborg," said the sheriff.

Ingeborg showed not the slightest sign of having understood what was going on, or what was about to happen.

"Would you let me pack her up a little something to eat?"

"By all means," replied the sheriff.

"I'll put in a piece of rye bread, some cured pork and a bottle of milk. That will do nicely, won't it, Ingeborg?" said Farmor, her voice trembling.

When she had finished getting it ready, she walked over to the table, placed the little bundle in Ingeborg's lap and patted her daughter-in-law on the cheek. Ingeborg did not respond, but continued staring out of the window.

"You have to go with the sheriff, my dear. Do you understand?"

Farmor took Ingeborg's arm to help her out of the chair. She asked her daughter to fetch Ingeborg's coat, and they both helped her put it on.

"Right then. Shall we get going?" asked the sheriff, who was waiting by the door.

He took Ingeborg by one arm, and Farmor took her other arm. They led her through the garden, past the apple tree, toward the telegraph pole on the main road to which the horse was tethered.

"Wait a minute!" cried Farmor when they were halfway there. "Let me give you a couple of bricks to take with you. I've warmed them on the stove."

She ran back into the house. The sheriff looked at his watch.

"Those are nice and warm to put under your feet," explained Farmor when she returned. "Ingeborg feels the cold."

The sheriff nodded.

"Now you shouldn't freeze during your journey," whispered Farmor, patting her daughter-in-law awkwardly on the shoulder.

Farmor stopped mid-gesture and held her hand to her mouth. She was frozen to the spot, as if standing to attention, holding the turned-up collar of her coat to protect herself from the icy blast. She was like the bare, straggly young birch trees outside the barn, bowed by the harsh wind. She waved to the departing wagon, but no-one waved back.

A dreadfully sad occurrence in the quiet village of Vesene. A mother drowned her three children in the washtub while her husband was out at work. Naturally this happened in a moment of insanity, the pastor wrote in his diary that evening.

The Prison Wagon

The square, yellow station building shone like gold in the setting sun. A lone man stood shivering at the gable end, lighting a cigarette and stamping his feet to keep warm.

"See to the horse and let the prison governor at Vänersborg know we're on our way," the sheriff told the clerk, as he helped Ingeborg out of the wagon.

They walked toward the entrance, where Ivar the pauper was sleeping at the foot of the steps. Ivar had acquired his name in the 1890s when he joined up as infantryman number 330 in the Elfsborg regiment. He had been pensioned off from the army a long time ago and now lived on poor relief.

"Somebody has been on a bender, I see," said the sheriff, poking the old man, who had a wild white beard.

"I must have missed my stop at Torpåkra," said Ivar with a groan.

"Indeed you must have," confirmed the sheriff. "But don't lie there and freeze to death, man. There's frost on the ground," he continued, holding open the door.

Ivar spat out his snuff and tottered into the warm waiting room. The freshly polished tile floor was gleaming. The sheriff and Ingeborg sat down on the wooden bench that ran along the wall, while Ivar stood opposite them, next to the stove.

"I've never known a winter to drag on as long as this. It will go down in history as the worst in living memory. Why on earth don't you go back home to your family?" said the sheriff.

"I have nobody left to go home to," sighed Ivar. "Did you not know that two of my children are already dead. My wee lassie died of the whooping cough before she was even four months old. And appendicitis took the lad when he was ten. But that's all a long time ago. The rest have been auctioned off or are slaving away as farmhands and housemaids in the parishes round about. The only one who has his life in order is my eldest son, who has followed in his father's footsteps and is now a sergeant major in the Stockholm regiment."

"But what about your wife, your eldest daughter and your grandchild," asked the sheriff.

"I'm better off without that old hag and the bastard. Anyhow, the council has put my missus in the madhouse in Gothenburg. They'll probably put me away soon, too. If only I had a cow! Then life would be worth living again."

The train puffed into the station, interrupting the conversation. The sheriff raised his hat in farewell and took Ingeborg by the arm. Ivar made himself comfortable on the bench, ready to sleep off the drink.

"Such a shame," said the sheriff, shaking his head.

Was he thinking of the hard-working navvy who had helped build the Älvsborg railway line before becoming Ivar the soldier and taking to the drink? Or was he thinking of Ingeborg, the young woman boarding the train in front of him, who could have been at home, tucking up her children in bed, instead of spending the rest of her life under lock and key?

The train departed on time. Fifteen minutes later, it reached Herrljunga, the junction with the main line. A cloud of black smoke greeted Ingeborg and the sheriff as they alighted onto the platform. A dusting of soot clung to the sweaty faces of the passengers hurrying past. The sheriff almost tripped over a couple of small boys sneaking beneath one of the carriages right in front of him.

"Are you out of your minds, boys?" he shouted. "What are you doing on the tracks? You could be crushed to death, you know, if the train starts moving any moment now!"

"We're just looking to see if the lads from Ljung have sent us any mail," said the boys, coming straight back clutching a dirty book.

The sheriff shook his head and muttered something about young people nowadays, as he spied an elegant gentleman with a cane on the platform, who smelled of shaving water and mothballs. The man was wearing a stiff fur cap that matched the collar of his double-breasted coat.

"Stationmaster Nenner, I presume?" said the sheriff, removing his black gloves to shake the man's hand.

"Correct."

"Good evening. My name is Sheriff Dahlstrand and this is…"

"Good evening," said the stationmaster, sticking his newspaper under his arm. "Do you read the *Allers Family Journal*, sheriff?"

"On occasion."

"Damn good paper. And a damn good article about smoking," said the stationmaster, blowing a smoke ring in Ingeborg's direction.

"As I was saying, this is…" said the sheriff.

"You had a pleasant journey, I trust?"

"Yes, it didn't take us long to get here. The next stage will be somewhat less pleasant for Mrs Andersson."

"I received a telephone call from the prison governor. No need to worry, sheriff. The custody officer will be here any minute."

The stationmaster looked at his pocket watch and tried to hide his irritation at the late arrival of the custody officer. The train was not due to leave until three minutes to six, but they had only twenty minutes to spare.

"We have plenty of time," he continued emphatically. "And the prison wagon has been ordered."

"Is that really necessary?" asked the sheriff.

"The prison wagon has provided excellent service for more than sixty years."

"So you are not acquainted with the new Criminal Justice Enforcement Act, then, stationmaster? Section 39 recommends that prisoners be transported with an escort in an ordinary passenger car."

"You need to speak up, sheriff," shouted the stationmaster as the prison wagon trundled in to platform two. "I can't hear you over the noise of the locomotive."

The exchange and transfer of prisoners began. The men were escorted across the station in groups. A streetwalker from Gothenburg was shoved back and forth between ragamuffins and well-dressed gentlemen.

"This is no place for young women," observed the sheriff.

"Young women? Whores, the lot of them! You're a soft touch, sheriff. Perhaps you should have gone into the church rather than the police?"

Eventually the custody officer turned up: a stout, middle-aged woman in uniform. With her grey, slicked-down hair severely centre-parted and pulled back in a bun, she appeared to be balding. Her white blouse was pulling at the neck, its top button concealed by an oval brooch.

The rust-red steel-plated wagon, built in 1868 and now coupled to the Vänersborg train, was small and dark, despite its wood-panelled interior having been freshly painted in light grey. Four individual cells were squeezed into one end of the wagon: two on each side of a gangway so narrow that the custody officer could not turn around and had to back out after escorting Ingeborg to her place at the far end. The rest of the wagon contained an earth closet and a shared cell to accommodate four low-risk prisoners. For security reasons, there was no corridor connection to the other carriages.

As the cell door slammed shut, Ingeborg sat down on the wooden bunk. For a moment, it seemed almost as dark as the root cellar at home. Only a weak shaft of light from the gaslights on the platform penetrated the barred opening in the roof. A stove was fixed to the floor beneath the seat, and Ingeborg leaned down to warm her hands.

"What, have you even insulated the attic?" she had asked when Artur showed her around what was to be their marital home for eight years.

"It's nowhere near as grand and well-appointed as my uncle's manor house, but the whole lot will be mine from the day I get married," Artur had replied earnestly, pointing out the wardrobes off the upstairs hall that he had turned into small bedrooms.

Ingeborg had run up to one of the slender mirrored doors, and then stopped suddenly and started swaying back and forth on the spot, beside herself with excitement.

"My big sister Ester is already married and is doing very nicely over at Klockaregården," Artur had continued after a long pause. "And my little sister Elsa can live with mother in the cottage. Provided she hasn't become too much of a princess while she was away in America. In which case Ester will surely take her in. My brother would probably like to keep his room here, of course. Do you think he could stay on? What do you say, Ingeborg?"

"Of course Holger can stay on. This is his home. He's such a nice, calm person."

"I'm so glad you like my brother," Artur had said.

Then they had stood in silence facing each other for a long while. Artur had tried to catch Ingeborg's gaze, but she was staring out of the window. She was fidgeting with her hands, rubbing them against each other, back and forth, as if she had washed them with too much soap and not managed to rinse off all the lather.

"Holger is a big help on the farm too," Artur had continued, before steeling himself to come out with the question that had been burdening him all week: "Will you marry me, Ingeborg?"

"Yes, Artur, I will. I so, so badly want to marry you," she had replied.

Some four hours later, Ingeborg found herself perched on the edge of a chair at a wide oak desk, opposite the governor of Vänersborg Penitentiary, who was filling in a form. His quill pen was scratching against the paper, causing the hairs on the back of her neck to stand up. The governor's white coat matched the white azalea, the sheets of paper in the bin and the unlit candle in its brass holder. Only the triangular letter scale in oxidized copper and a tall crank telephone in hardwood and bakelite with golden fittings clashed with the sterile colour palette. At regular intervals, the governor peered over the top of his glasses, dipped his pen in the black ink and looked searchingly at Ingeborg.

Silent, brooding and withdrawn, apathetic and languid, he wrote in the ledger to describe the new inmate.

The governor's assistant counted Ingeborg's money and searched the travel bag she had brought with her. He rifled and rummaged through her belongings before pulling them out one at a time. On a nod from the governor, he stuffed them back in. The registration process was complete.

Inmate No.	119
Arrival date	March 22, 1929, 10:10 p.m.
Category	1
Occupation	Wife
Physical characteristics	Height 167 cm
	Brown hair
	Blue eyes
	Oval face
	Straight nose
	Regular build
Clothing	1 x Boa
	1 pair Galoshes
	1 pair Underpants
	1 x Coat
	2 x Skirts
	1 x Dress
	1 x Cardigan
	1 pair Boots
	1 x Linen gown
	1 x Handkerchief
	1 x Sweater
	1 x Blanket
Cash	6 kronor 60 öre

The governor read through the information and reached for a rotating metal stand holding seven stamps. Finding the one he required, he applied the imprint before sliding the heavy, brown, cardboard-covered ledger across the desk with one hand, while handing Ingeborg a pen with the other.

"Life, what's the point of it?" thought Ingeborg as the letters on the page all merged into one another before her eyes.

The governor tapped his quill pen impatiently on the desk a couple of times.

"Please sign here," he said, pointing to the dotted line at the foot of the page in the prison register:

I certify that all cash and other belongings that accompanied me on arrival have been correctly listed and valued above.

The governor's handwriting was almost illegible, but the information was surely correct. During the police interview back home, Ingeborg had compliantly answered yes or no to all the sheriff's questions. She was not going to start arguing now. She took the pen and signed, with trembling hand: *Ingeborg Andersson*.

The Trial

Ingeborg was sitting in the back seat of a tall, rectangular car. It was not the beer truck, nor the milk truck. It was a Volvo with a three-speed gearbox, a black pegamoid roof and an ash wood chassis. The inhabitants of Ljung had braved the rain to step outside for a glimpse of the latest model proudly produced by the Gothenburg factory, with a top speed of a hundred kilometres an hour.

It was ten o'clock in the morning on April 5, 1929. The chauffeur, a young man dressed in collar and tie and a cap with a stiff, shiny brim, pulled into the entrance to the Gäsene courthouse, stepped out of the car, and opened the door for the custody officer, who ordered Ingeborg to get out.

Ingeborg did not respond, and the woman eventually lost patience. Her family had been in the service of crown and state for generations. Used to being obeyed, she leaned in, grabbed Ingeborg under the arm, and dragged her captive out of the car, over the large rear mudguard. Ingeborg stared at the ground, covering her face with her hand to avoid the prying eyes lurking behind the windowpanes of the courthouse's glazed veranda. Her dark grey woollen coat was trailing on the ground. An elderly couple stood in line at the entrance.

"So that's what she looks like," said the man as Ingeborg and the custody officer walked past.

"She's not in shackles, whatever were they thinking?" said the woman, who had been reading the newspaper especially carefully for the past two weeks.

The interior had a low ceiling, and Ingeborg instinctively bowed her head. She walked past the downstairs room with an open hearth where the peasants used to dry off their shoes after trudging to court. With great effort, Ingeborg mounted the stone stairs leading up to the courtroom, propelled from behind by the custody officer.

The court was packed with curious observers from the local villages and beyond. The damp heat clung to chairs and tables, walls and ceilings, in a venue where defendants were more usually on trial for the illegal production and sale of liquor. Never before had the judge been called upon to try a murderess.

Among those sitting in the front row were the cobbler from Slätthult and Kristina from Kyrkefalla. Ivar from Vesene, dressed in his old rags, had also found a seat there. Artur was sitting between Mother Selma and Farmor. The local scuttlebutt was that Farmor had been involved with a Mexican when she was away in America. That was why Artur and his siblings were so swarthy, they claimed. But that story was nothing compared to what they now had to gossip about.

Ingeborg walked toward the chair next to the judge's desk at the front of the podium. She almost lost her balance as the ground started to sway beneath her.

"Here we are," said the custody officer, taking hold of her. "Just a few steps to go now."

Ingeborg shuffled the last few steps like a sleepwalker. She collapsed on one side of the wooden chair, folded up her legs beneath her and hunched up, in order not to occupy more space than necessary. The custody officer helped her off with her pillbox hat, but didn't manage to get her coat off. Ingeborg had assumed a pose with her arms crossed, rocking her upper body back and forth while incessantly rubbing her palms against her elbows inside her coat.

The custody officer stuffed her handkerchief into the sleeve of Ingeborg's coat and nodded a brief goodbye — as if, in her cold, stern way, she was wishing her charge good luck, saying that everything would work out in the end. Ingeborg grabbed the handkerchief and began fidgeting with its lace edge, turning it round and round and round.

The seamstress back home had draped similar lace around Ingeborg's waist when she tried on her wedding dress for the first time. She had been perched on a wooden bench outside the cottage because it was far too dark and cramped indoors. Mother Selma had sent Ingeborg's elder sister to keep watch at the gate, to make sure no passing villagers happened to witness the event.

"It's beautiful, that's for sure," her mother had said with a sigh, feeling the train of fine chiffon. "But you don't want it to be too showy."

The seamstress had crouched at Ingeborg's feet to pin up the front hem to ankle height, so that the shoes would be visible. Before setting to work with needle and thread, she had asked Ingeborg to spin around a couple of times, so she could check the hem was even.

"The hem has to be shorter at the front," she had explained. "That's the latest thing."

"Don't freak the girl out. We can't let her strut around like that and become a laughing stock."

"Freak her out?" the seamstress had repeated, berating her old friend. "Don't be so silly! Go and put the coffee on instead of standing there pontificating about fashions you don't understand."

The seamstress had taken Ingeborg's hand in her own and stroked the bitten cuticles.

"On your wedding day I'll lend you a pair of long white gloves with mother-of-pearl buttons."

Next to Ingeborg sat Attorney Lundberg, whom the county authorities had appointed as counsel for the defence. Lundberg, from Vänersborg, was a member of the Swedish Bar Association. At the large oak desk, the presiding judge for the Borås circuit sat in splendid isolation, in a high-backed, ornamented wood chair with a dark red velvet seat. A pale, lean man with a good head of hair, he picked distractedly at his long fingernails while waiting for the courtroom murmur to subside. A white handkerchief protruded from the left breast pocket of his jacket. Behind the presiding judge, on a wooden bench in front of the large windows, sat Magistrate Svensson and six lay judges. Six earnest men in black three-piece suits, white shirts and black ties, chosen to represent the local communities, from Fåglavik in the north to Mollaryd in the south, from Ljurhalla in the west to Vimle in the east. The senior circuit notary sat farthest to the right, pen and paper in his lap, ready to record the proceedings.

"Silence in court!" cried the judge, banging his gavel. "I hereby declare the proceedings open," he continued when the noise had abated.

Attorney Frändén, counsel for the prosecution, rose to his feet and began his submission by outlining the defendant's personal details to the court:

"Mrs Ingeborg Maria Andersson, née Olsson, born June 14, 1901, in the parish of Vesene, has no criminal record. She is the daughter of August Olsson, farmer, and his wife Selma, who currently have dispensation to occupy Aläng farm in the parish of Vesene. The defendant has three brothers and three sisters, all of whom have reached the age of majority. Except for one sister, the defendant's siblings are all older than her. Some of them live with their parents, while others are married. The defendant attended elementary school in Vesene and is able to read and write. She was confirmed at the age of fourteen at Södra Björke parish church, having passed her religious knowledge examination. Since June 22, 1923, she has been married to Artur Ejnar Andersson, farmer. The marriage has produced three children: Tor Ingvar, born April 9, 1924, Anders Artur Efraim, born January 10, 1926, and Inga Britta Lucia, born December 13, 1927."

As the dead children's names were read out, there was a commotion among the audience, and the judge again had to bang his gavel.

"Silence in court!"

The prosecutor described the interviews conducted with Ingeborg, her husband and mother, her in-laws and her midwife. He described all the unanswered questions and the postmortem examination of the children at home. The floorboards creaked as he handed over the documents to the notary and confirmed that he had nothing to add for the time being.

"What is your first name?" asked the judge in an awe-inspiring voice to begin his examination.

Ingeborg stared straight ahead without responding.

"What is your first name?" repeated the judge, crossing his smooth hands on the desk in front of him while the villagers shifted on the court benches. "Could you tell us your first name please, madam?"

"Andersson," replied Ingeborg.

"I was asking for your first name. Are you troubled by the presence of all these spectators, Mrs Andersson?"

Ingeborg was holding on to the handkerchief so hard that her knuckles were white. She breathed deeply as the judge ordered the courtroom to be cleared. From time to time she rolled her eyes. With tense jaw muscles and slightly flushed cheeks, she then replied that her name was Ingeborg and she had recently turned twenty-seven. She could not remember the year of her marriage, but she did remember that it was a church wedding.

"What a beautiful wedding!" Mother Selma had exclaimed as they returned home down the avenue of bright green ash trees. "You're so fortunate, Ingeborg! The Almighty is kind."

The flag had been raised, and ninety-two guests were posing in front of the twin ceremonial arches made from spruce branches.

"Why so serious, folks? You look like you've been to a funeral," said the photographer before firing the flash. "Now let's take one of just the groomsmen. How many of you are there? One, two, three… fourteen! And now let's pull up some chairs for the bridesmaids. Sit down in a row in front of the lads, with your hands in your lap. Like that. How about a little smile?"

Farmor had welcomed the guests and invited them to enjoy the buffet in the parlour, where three long tables lined up against the walls were laden with six kinds of canapés, broth with pastries, haddock and boiled potatoes, roast veal with all the trimmings, and bread and baked cheese. The linen tablecloths were freshly mangled, and the oxeye daisies were resplendent.

"Please tuck in, before it gets cold."

"I'm family, so I can't go first," muttered Mother Selma, staying put in the kitchen.

"But you're the oldest," insisted Farmor, but Mother Selma continued to stand on ceremony.

"I can't go ahead of the pastor!"

"Are you a member of the Pentecostal church, Mrs Andersson?" The judge continued his questioning, but Ingeborg did not hear him.

"Are you hiding away here with the old ladies?" Artur had asked when he came into the kitchen and embraced her.

Ingeborg, who had a mouthful of chocolate, had nearly choked.

"The air is so thick with smoke you could cut it with a knife," complained Farmor. "We'll have to ventilate the place thoroughly this evening, otherwise you won't get a wink of sleep tonight."

"What he needs is a good strong coffee laced with something," cried one of the old men in the adjoining room.

"And so it goes on," said Mother Selma, glancing through the doorway. "Now the hip flask is coming out."

"Artur, why don't you get out the couronne game and take the worst of the rowdies outside with you?" Farmor had suggested. "It's a lovely warm evening. Then we women can start clearing up. Otherwise I fear the dishwasher will have to stay overnight."

Ingeborg had gone upstairs with Artur to fetch the square board game with a hole in each corner. The old men from the neighbouring farms had each taken their cue and then bickered over who was to have the red rings, because the black ones were unlucky. They were starting to get drunk and couldn't really handle the game.

Once the sun had set, Artur lit the coloured glass and paper lanterns that his sisters had strung up in the garden earlier in the day. An old schoolmate was riding a bicycle round and round the well lever.

"Be careful with Ingeborg's bike, damn it!" Artur yelled.

He thought his friend was going home to fetch more liquor, but the friend was not listening and headed out for a spin on the main road. On his return, he fell off and landed in the ditch.

"Bloody hell, you've got lots of nettles here!" he exclaimed when he was back on his feet.

"Serves you right, I'd say," replied Artur, and they both roared with laughter.

"I asked if you were a member of the Pentecostal church," repeated the judge.

"No," replied Ingeborg.

Artur's old schoolmate had cycled home to fetch some fireworks and lit up the summer night with a spectacular display.

He let off fourteen fireworks in such rapid succession that his hands were covered in gunpowder. Red, white, green and purple comets illuminated the sky for a few seconds before falling back to earth in an explosive cascade.

The judge persisted: "The meeting house is only a short distance from your home. Have you really never attended a Pentecostal meeting or brooded over matters of religion?"

"No."

"So how come you have been so quiet and withdrawn lately, as your relatives have stated?"

Ingeborg had heard the postman's horn and gone to the parlour window. Through the net curtains, she had watched the postman dismount from his bicycle for a chat with the midwife. He was wearing a short jacket with epaulettes and shiny buttons. He was probably talking about sorting the mail over at Månsen's house, which served as the village post office because the postman was illiterate. Perhaps he was saying how almost all the letters were sent home with the schoolchildren, but because Tor, Efraim and Lucia were not yet of school age, he had to cycle over to the Anderssons' with their mail. The midwife, who had delivered Ingeborg's three children, had leaned her bicycle against the fence. She nodded goodbye to the postman as he went on his way. Smoothing out her nurse's uniform with both hands, she walked slowly up the gravel path to the house.

"Mother Selma asked me to look in on her daughter," she said when the nurserymaid opened the door.

"Mrs Andersson has just popped out. May I offer you a cup of coffee while you wait?"

The nurserymaid was a sensible girl from Vänersborg who did as she was told.

"Yes, please," replied the midwife, pointing to Lucia. "The little one is getting big."

"She'll be a year old in a couple of months, on Saint Lucia's day."

Ingeborg heard the midwife sit down on one of the kitchen chairs. She heard the nurserymaid take Efraim through to the bedroom and ask Tor to look after his little brother for a while, before setting out the cups and taking the coffee pan off the stove.

The judge continued his examination: "Have you been suffering from vomiting, indigestion or anything like that?"

"No," replied Ingeborg.

Mother Selma had blabbed about Ingeborg's hemorrhoids to the midwife, who in turn told the nurserymaid. But the nurserymaid gave her short shrift:

"I know nothing about any hemorrhoids, but Mrs Andersson has lost a lot of weight since Liss passed away, and she is not sleeping well. Both of us are having trouble sleeping, in fact."

"I just hope Ingeborg hasn't inherited her father's weak nerves. He's taken to his bed again and hasn't got up for several months. Mother Selma really isn't having an easy time of it!"

"Mr Andersson has tried making an appointment to see the doctor, but Mrs Andersson won't go."

"If Ingeborg is embarrassed to go to the village doctor, I could have a word with Dr Segelberg in Borås. Is Mr Andersson at home?"

"No, he's gone to the woods with his brother and the farmhand."

"Then you must tell Ingeborg to take it easy. If she doesn't put some weight back on, she could get really sick," the midwife had said before cycling away.

"Mrs Andersson, did you have any reason to be jealous, or was your husband violent, on the morning of March 22, 1929?" asked the judge.

Ingeborg could not have found a better husband than Artur. Mother Selma had worried unnecessarily when Artur began courting Ingeborg at the age of twenty. Selma thought she knew what going to those wretched dance halls could lead to. What's more, Artur was a prosperous landowning farmer and was seven years older. Ingeborg's father, on the other hand, thought Artur was a fine fellow and urged Selma to let the girl enjoy a fling after all her toil around the house.

Ingeborg recalled the morning when Artur came pedalling up the forest road on a new bicycle with large balloon tyres and wooden handlebars. Her father, who was clearing brushwood, raised the brim of his cap with two fingers in acknowledgment. But Artur went over to greet him properly, forcing him to wipe his fingers clean on his trouser leg before shaking Artur's outstretched hand.

"Good day to you! I take it my future son-in-law has come a-courting out in this neck of the woods?" Ingeborg's father had joked.

As he spoke, a thin line of snuff dribbled out of the right corner of his mouth onto his furrowed face.

"How are things?" inquired Artur, propping the bicycle against the red-painted outhouse.

"Not so bad, thanks. Could be better, could be worse. Just a shame you get so knackered when you reach my age. Probably because you overdid it in your younger days and have gone and worn yourself out."

"You need to take it easy, uncle."

"Yes, bed is always a good place. But you can't stay there all the time."

"What have you done with Ingeborg?" asked Artur. "I came bearing birthday greetings."

"That's wonderful. We appreciate it. She's working away in there," said the old man, pointing at the steps with the scythe shaft.

"Happy birthday, my love!" Artur had cried as he ran toward the cottage. "I went to market last Tuesday to buy fodder cakes, and on my way home I spotted that bicycle in the shop window."

"Artur, my dear, you shouldn't have! It must have been terribly expensive!"

"Don't you like it?"

"Of course I like it! It's the nicest present I've ever been given!"

The sun glinted off the bicycle's silver frame, almost blinding Ingeborg when she gently placed her hand on the soft seat.

"I just need to adjust the handlebars, then you can go for a test drive."

"That will be such fun! You spoil me terribly!"

"This is just the beginning, Ingeborg, just the beginning," Artur had said as he embraced her.

The judge interrupted Ingeborg's thoughts: "Had you previously ever thought about taking the lives of your children?"

"No."

"What were your innermost feelings as you watched the children writhing and struggling to break free?"

"I don't know. It came to me on a whim."

"Did you not think that your actions were unjust and felonious? Do you not regret killing your children?"

"No."

The judge brought the proceedings to a close, and the notary recorded:

In view of events in the case, the court deems it necessary to obtain the opinion of the National Board of Medicine with regard to the defendant's mental state at the time of committing the acts with which she is charged; consequently, the case files are to be forwarded to the National Board of Medicine and the case is stayed pending receipt of the requested opinion, and meanwhile Ingeborg Andersson is remanded in custody.

Cotton and Burlap

Ingeborg kept her coat on throughout the train journey from Vänersborg to Växjö. Leaning forward slightly, she sat without support, staring down at the floor. Just as rigid, just as silent, hour after hour. She was the only prisoner in the compartment. The custody officer was much shorter and stronger than Ingeborg, but perhaps people could still have taken them for a mother and daughter on a Saturday evening outing.

One Saturday in June of 1927, Ingeborg had travelled by train with Artur and Liss to Falköping, where the Cirkus Strassberger from Germany was performing. Tor was three years old, and Efraim was one. Ingeborg was three months pregnant with Lucia. Her sister, who had lived with them and looked after the boys up until then, had got into trouble and had had to get married. To a good man, it must be said, but unlike Artur he was not the eldest son, and so they had set up home in another village.

At first, Artur had wanted to take Tor to the circus with them to celebrate Liss's birthday. It was true that Liss helped Ingeborg's husband in the woods, when he was not working at the sawmill in Axelfors, but he was *her* eldest nephew. There was not much of an age gap between them, and Ingeborg looked on him as a cousin, a brother almost. They had grown up together.

But Ingeborg had objected when she saw the price of the tickets advertised on the poster depicting the round, striped tent surrounded by wagons containing wild animals. She told Artur he was pampering his children, that he could not spend that sort of money on a child who would not remember anything about it anyway. Ingeborg had got her way, but Tor had cried and Artur had consoled him, picking him up for a hug and promising him all kinds of good things when they returned. Before leaving, he had held his son high in the air and spun around several times, just as he used to pick Ingeborg up and spin her around when they first fell in love.

"Here we are," said the custody officer.

The yellow stuccoed station building in the Swiss chalet style loomed against the twilit sky as the train pulled in to the platform. The custody officer donned her dark blue ulster, and the two women alighted.

A band had been playing on a stage in front of the big top when they arrived in Falköping. A llama was lazing in a blue wagon in the summer heat. In another wagon, a lion cub was playing. Artur had bought Ingeborg a big ice cream, but she had been so engrossed in watching all the jugglers and clowns that she had forgotten all about it. The chocolate had melted and trickled down the cone. She searched her handbag for a handkerchief but could not find one.

"I've got a napkin here," a slim teenage girl standing next to them in line had said.

After they had gone up the ramp and it turned out that the girl had the seat next to him, Liss had held his hand over his chin to hide his sparse, stubbly beard and put on an exaggerated display of enthusiasm.

Ingeborg and the prisoners from the other cars were assembled in the station yard and each given a thin, white linen mask that covered their head and neck. During their imprisonment, they had to be protected from the influence of hardened repeat offenders. The masks were also intended to protect them from the public; no-one would recognize them when they were released after serving their sentences. Through hard work, and with God's help, they would be reformed and given the opportunity for a fresh start, a new, free life away from the judgmental gazes of others.

Ingeborg caught sight of her reflection in the windows of the station building. A pair of eyes she did not recognize stared back at her through the two large, round, edge-stitched holes in the mask. She recalled the clowns at the circus with their false noses and grotesque makeup. The stunt artist scuttling around behind the elephant in the ring and pretending to trip over a stool, and then running in zigzag fashion like a drunk, before falling headlong into the sawdust. It was no laughing matter.

Ingeborg and the other prisoners filed through Växjö city centre like some medieval order. A seven-minute walk of shame from the station through Båtmanstorget and past the Lundgren's Snuff building, up Bäckgatan and past the wooden shanties on Teatertorget. Ingeborg was leading the procession, and after a couple of blocks she spied the large stone building behind a solid wall at the top of the hill.

In front of the stone gateway stood a woman who was waving. Superintendent Lillie Appelgren was in charge of routine paperwork and supplies at the prison, and oversaw the examination and registration of all new inmates. In her white apron and light blue, longsleeved blouse, she looked like a young nurse, although she had been working at the prison for almost twenty years. Her heavily starched collar was fastened with a brooch. Her brown hair was gathered up in a bun, but some of her locks were coming loose in the wind, and strands of soft, fine hair were curling around her face and forehead.

"Welcome to Växjö," she said, unlocking the door. "I hope your journey was not too arduous."

The custody officer took custody slip number 593 out of her pocket and handed it to the superintendent, who nodded and read it.

Officer Anna Jonsson is hereby instructed to escort by special prisoner transport Mrs Ingeborg Maria Andersson, who has been arrested and charged with murder, from Vänersborg Penitentiary to Växjö Central Penitentiary on April 20, 1929, and to deliver the accused into the custody of the latter institution, in exchange for the requisite receipt, for investigation of the accused's mental state pursuant to the order issued by the National Board of Corrections on April 15, 1929.

The female prison officers wore black felt moccasins and moved noiselessly over the wide floorboards. Once the custody officers had departed, the large entrance hall fell strangely silent. Only the rattling of the superintendent's bunch of keys, a steel ring holding about ten keys of various sizes, reminded the women of where they were.

Sweden's seventy-four female prisoners were held here. Twenty-three of them had been convicted of theft, fourteen of criminal abortion, eleven of fraud and forgery, five of child murder, four of prostitution, and two each of arson, procuring and illegal dealing in liquor.

The prisoners were not allowed to converse among themselves, and when they left their cells, for instance for their daily walk or weekly lessons, they had to wear their masks. The building was designed to prevent communication and physical contact, but the long-standing inmates had learned to communicate by knocking on their cell walls.

The superintendent led the way to the admission room on the main floor. The administrative part of the building was heated by tiled stoves, which combined with the range in the adjacent kitchen to create a pleasantly warm ambience. The rest of the prison was heated by pipes in the floor connected to a central heating plant in the basement, where the dark cells used for solitary confinement were also located.

"It's late, and you must be tired after your long journey," said the superintendent, producing some prison clothing. "We can postpone the obligatory bath until the morning."

Ingeborg handed over her clothes and put on a cotton jersey nightgown and a pair of big, coarse cotton underpants that were kept up by a drawstring at the waist. The nightgown had been carefully mended and patched, and one of its white buttons had come off and been replaced by a zinc button.

The superintendent accompanied Ingeborg up an open spiral staircase to her cell. The interior of the prison resembled an atrium, with large skylights and an open central hall extending from the basement to the third storey. High above them, a corridor guard stood watch on a gangway spanning the central hall. Everything turned black before Ingeborg's eyes, and she grabbed hold of the banister. Against the light, the corridor guard resembled the tightrope walker in a black leotard at the Cirkus Strassberger, who had balanced on a steel wire with a red rose in her mouth, performed a pirouette and then done the splits when she reached the end of the tightrope.

The ringmaster had spoken a foreign language, but Ingeborg had understood to keep quiet. She held her breath as the spotlight focused on a swing suspended from the tent ceiling. A muscular man with a bare torso was swinging slowly back and forth in a kneeling position, ready at the right moment to catch the acrobat who came flying through the air. Ingeborg could hardly bring herself to watch as the flying man performed a double somersault.

After the trapeze act, it was time for the equestrian vaulting. An unsaddled horse, with its head held high and feathers decorating the headband of the bridle, had galloped round and round until Ingeborg was dizzy. After a short run-up, the rider had leapt onto the horse's back and performed a handstand, holding on to the metal rings in the belly band.

"We'll have to try that at home with Blaze," Liss had said, and all three of them had laughed.

"You can come to the infirmary as soon as a place becomes free for you, Ingeborg," said the superintendent as they reached the second floor, where the recently established department for women undergoing psychiatric evaluation was located.

The middle floor also contained the prison governor's residence, comprising three rooms and a kitchen, and the superintendent's apartment. They walked past the cells lining the outer walls, of which there were about thirty on each floor. Eighty of the cells were allocated to the women's penitentiary and ten to the infirmary, the superintendent explained. The cells were all slightly different in width and were arranged in a staggered pattern so that the inmates could not see their counterpart on the other side of the central hall if the doors or food hatches happened to be open at the same time. Suddenly, there was the sound of a child crying, and Ingeborg gave a start.

"Don't be frightened, Mrs Andersson," said the superintendent. "We have a lot of babies here. This year alone, three mothers have given birth. They are housed over here in the infants' room. Myself and the janitor are godparents to little Astrid, who was born last week."

The girl at the circus was named Astrid too. She had been given a ticket by her employer in compensation for lost wages. Her boss had gone bankrupt, but apparently knew one of the acrobats. After the performance, the girl had kept them company on their walk back to the station. She was heading home to her mother in Vänersborg to look for a new job. Artur had asked what kind of work she was interested in, and it turned out she was a nurserymaid with good references.

"Just look at that! She's like a gift from on high, don't you think, Ingeborg?" Artur had said, giving the girl their telephone number.

The new nurserymaid had started work the following week. She was a sensible girl.

The superintendent unlocked Ingeborg's cell. The solid wooden door had two hatches and a peephole: a small hatch for talking to the guards and a larger food hatch. The peephole was no larger than a five-öre piece.

"And now, Mrs Andersson, it's time for you to try and get some sleep," said the superintendent, closing the door.

The twin bolts dropped automatically into place as the superintendent turned the key in the lock. Ingeborg was left standing inside the cell, facing the back of the bolted door, on which the prison rules were posted.

NOTICE TO INMATES. *The following actions will be severely* ***punished: defacing*** *of books, walls, doors, floors, commodes, basin lids, tables, chairs, stools, beds, dishes and cups, soap dishes, spittoons, and any other furnishings and fixtures that may be present in the cell;* ***staining or soiling of the walls; insertion of pins or needles into and removal of threads from*** *apparel, bedclothes or towels; and* ***any other careless use*** *of furnishings, fixtures or clothing. Furthermore, any inmate found to have damaged books or other furnishings and fixtures in the cell will be liable for the costs of replacement.*

My Dear little Artur
now I am waiting for a letter please dont let me wait in vain you are so very kind I am coming home to you soon time is passing so quick
   I get a bath every tuesday
   Heartfelt greetings and much love to you all at Haggården
   just imagin if I could come to you with this letter Ive been thinking my home is not on Erth it is above the clouds Ingeborg
   when you write my adress write this instead then you dont have to write Prison infirmary is what it says on all them other letters
To 26/29
Norra Esplanaden
22 Växjö

In Lonely Moments

Condensation from the windowpane drained into two grooves on the wide sill below. A bestial howl interrupted the monotonous sound of drips hitting the bottom of the zinc collection tray.

"Damn the lot of you!" yelled a woman farther down the corridor. "I don't want to be here!"

Ingeborg pulled the pillow over her head, hugging it tightly with both arms in an attempt to shut out the heartrending sound and the woman's foul language.

"Shut it, you old bag!" yelled another inmate.

Ingeborg was shaking all over and praying to God that they would stop. Over and over again, she rattled off her bedtime prayer. Eventually she heard rapid footsteps hurrying down the corridor.

"Now then!"

The superintendent's calm voice was interrupted by more complaints. Ranting and raving, the woman was escorted downstairs to the basement. Ingeborg wailed under the covers. She wiped away her tears with the back of her right hand, trying not to soak the pillowcase. Her eyes had started to swell. Her face felt soft and puffy, as if it was about to dissolve. Her nose was running, but it was dark and she didn't dare get out of bed to find a new handkerchief. The one in her hand was soaking wet. The snivelling and her uneven breathing convulsed her body like spasms.

"Be quiet, woman!" shouted the inmate in the next cell, banging on the wall.

Ingeborg clamped her mouth shut to stop the sobbing, biting her lip so hard she made it bleed. She quickly licked the blood away so as not to stain the prison bedding.

It was starting to get light, and Ingeborg cautiously opened her eyes to peek around the bleak, bare cell. The lower half of the walls was painted sky blue, the upper half pale yellow. The two colours were separated by an inch-thick black band level with the windowsill. On one of the long walls there was a tapestry of a red cottage with the motto *Diligence is Fortune's right hand*.

Ingeborg got out of bed and bent down to lift the hasp and open the wooden lid of the small rectangular cupboard on the floor. The heavy orange ceramic basin with its two small lugs resembled one of those large flowerpots that grand folk often had in their garden. Ingeborg was about to lift out the chamber pot when the auxiliary guard opened the second hatch on the cupboard from the corridor side. Ingeborg quickly slammed the hatch shut on her side, suddenly realizing that she had forgotten to pour a scoop of water into the pot the previous night. How could she forget? The last thing she had done before going to bed was to read the instructions. The tears welled up in her throat.

Inmates must attend to any calls of nature at the designated location during their time in the prison yard. The chamber pot is to be used only for urine and in the event of sudden nausea during the night. After use of the pot in the latter circumstances, a spoonful of chalk must be sprinkled in the pot and the lid must be closed quickly, in order to prevent the release of unsanitary odours into the cell, after which the drain in the lid must be filled with water to at least the halfway point. The drain in the lid must never be without water even if the pot is empty.

The time was almost half past seven, and Ingeborg could hear the breakfast tray being placed on the folding table outside the cell, just as the larger hatch in the door was opened. When Ingeborg did not come forward to accept the bowl of oatmeal gruel, the bread roll and the milk, a nurse opened the cell door.

"Good morning, Mrs Andersson! My name is Sister Gunhild," said the young woman, setting down the food on the table. "I hope you will fancy this."

"Hope you fancy it." That was what Artur had said, too, when he brought her breakfast in bed the morning after their wedding.

Ingeborg had been woken by the rattle of cups in the kitchen and a coffee smell seeping under the bedroom door, but pretended to be asleep when Artur entered the room and sat down on the edge of the bed beside her. When he stroked her cheek, she sat up and fiddled with the sheets, running her fingers over the soft embroidered monogram in mouliné thread.

"Oh, how lovely!" she had whispered when she saw the tray decorated with newly picked violets. "Where did you get hold of freshly baked pastries at this time of day?"

"The shopkeeper brought them out here this morning. I ordered them ages ago," Artur had replied.

The stream of coffee had made a tinkling sound as it hit the bottom of the tin mug when Artur poured it from the silver coffee pot that Farmor had given them as a wedding present.

"The chaplain is here to welcome you to Växjö, Mrs Andersson," Sister Gunhild continued, introducing a man with slicked-down hair parted at the side and dressed in a long, black, closely fitting cassock.

"My condolences on the sad loss of your children, you poor woman," said the chaplain, entering the room and extending his hand. "I bring the word of the Lord."

The chaplain sat down on the stool and looked around the cell. He picked up a dark green volume from Ingeborg's table, with the title *In Lonely Moments* printed in ornate gold letters on the cover. The chaplain turned to the first page and started reading:

DEAR READER, so it has come to this and you now find yourself here. Perhaps for a while you have not been entirely unprepared for this, as you felt that things were 'going downhill' and realized that the path you had chosen would lead to misfortune and sorrow. Your suspicions that it would end badly have now been proven correct. The reasons for your present situation are best known to yourself, and in your innermost self you will surely admit that, to be honest, it was your alienation from God that was the cause of your misfortune.

The thin book was well worn, and both covers had been repaired with extra-strong sewing thread to keep the pages in place.

"I see you already have the Bible and a hymn book, Mrs Andersson," said the chaplain when he had finished reading the first paragraph of Pastor Salvén's message to Sweden's prison inmates. "That is good. I shall leave you this book as well. Under the rules, you are not allowed to borrow any other books from the prison library in your first two months here."

Sister Gunhild returned to collect the breakfast tray. When the chaplain had left, she unhooked the drip tray from the wires in the window and emptied the water into the chamber pot. On her way out, she almost collided with a strongly-built man in his sixties.

"Oops, that could have been bad," said the man, who had bushy eyebrows.

The tips of the man's moustache were waxed and slightly upturned. His thick, dark hair was neatly back-combed in the middle, resembling a high toupee. His white coat was tight around the middle, and the cuffs of his jacket protruded from the sleeves. Although the doctor was already standing in the doorway, he knocked gently on the inside of Ingeborg's door before sticking his head in.

"May I come in?"

Ingeborg was semi-reclined in bed, wearing the white prison nightgown. The cotton fabric was discoloured around the armholes with sweat from the inmates who had worn it previously.

"Mrs Andersson arrived on Saturday and has stayed in bed since. For three days. She does not respond when spoken to," whispered Sister Gunhild. "The prison doctor at Vänersborg ordered her transfer to the infirmary, but we have no room," she sighed.

"I shall see what I can do," replied the doctor, before turning to his patient.

Ingeborg was staring straight ahead. She showed no sign of having noticed that someone had entered the room. She folded her hands to make them stop shaking. When that did not work, she began scratching at her forearms.

"My name is Dr Goldkuhl and I have been the physician-in-charge here at the prison for thirty years," said the man, extending his hand in greeting only for it to be left hanging in mid-air.

He pulled a navy blue tin bearing the Swedish royal warrant out of his pocket and put a tablet in his mouth. The aroma of menthol filled the small cell.

"Would you like to try a Pix, Mrs Andersson?" Dr Goldkuhl continued, holding out the tin of white pastilles. "How are you feeling today?"

Dr Goldkuhl took two steps across to the other side of the room, sat down on the rickety stool between the table and the bedhead, next to Ingeborg, and waited for an answer. When he received none, he opened up her chart and started silently reading the findings of the physical examination performed by his colleague at Vänersborg Penitentiary.

Slender build, no deformities or defects, flesh and musculature barely ordinary. 164 centimetres, 53.5 kilograms. Overall complexion normal, countenance somewhat pale, transparent with dark rings below eyes. Face, neck and upper thorax easily become flushed. Moderate dermatographia. Face well formed, eyebrows not coalesced, earlobes solid. Hair ash blond. Eyesight and hearing good. Eye movements coordinated. Pupil dilation medium, photosensitivity normal. Retinae unremarkable. Tongue and oral cavity generally unremarkable, but dentition poor with caries in a number of teeth.

The doctor looked up from the chart at the barred window high on the exterior wall. With some effort, when the sun clouded over, he could make out the top of the tall birch tree on the far side of the prison yard.

"Have you noticed that the leaves are starting to bud, Mrs Andersson?" he asked. "Spring must be here at last."

It was meant to be an ordinary comment, the opening line of an informal conversation — small talk intended to build trust. He was usually good at this sort of thing, but when he came to the end of the sentence he recognized his stupidity. His patient no longer cared about the weather and the changing seasons. Ingeborg's psychiatric examination was scheduled for June 30. He had little more than two months to win the trust of this silent, terrified country girl. He carried on reading the chart.

Heart unremarkable, pulse regular, rate varies according to situation, generally raised. Lungs unremarkable. Abdomen unremarkable. Liver and spleen not palpable. Hands and feet somewhat cold and damp. External genitalia unremarkable. Some small hemorrhoidal knots in anus. Urine free of sugar and albumin. Tendon/periosteal reflexes in arms and knee/heel reflexes lively. Babinski neg. Romberg neg. Sense of pain and touch unremarkable. Muscle sense unremarkable. Stools good. Menstruation not occurred. Afebrile temperature.

Dr Goldkuhl closed the chart and was pleased that his new patient at least appeared to be in good physical health. The risk of tuberculosis seemed to be over, as the number of cases was falling steadily across the country. In the first six months of the year, only two of the inmates in his care had died of the dreaded lung disease. Typhoid was not claiming many victims anymore either, since he had introduced vaccination for all new arrivals. Influenza, however, was a real problem. Almost a quarter of the inmates and staff had been infected, but Ingeborg had avoided it so far.

Dr Goldkuhl noticed the three books on the wall shelf in the corner.

"Do you like reading, Mrs Andersson?" he asked, squeezing the thin, dark green book with gold lettering that was out on the table.

"God has forsaken me," whispered Ingeborg without looking up.

"I shouldn't think so," replied the doctor. "You mustn't believe everything that Pastor Salvén writes. Tomorrow, I shall bring you something more enjoyable from the library, Ingeborg."

On arrival the patient was very run down both physically and mentally, wrote Dr Goldkuhl on Ingeborg's chart, prescribing an opium treatment for heavy depression.

Saturday May 4th 1929

My Dear Artur

it was so nice to get a letter I was waiting for a letter I was so sad I thought you were coming to see me on sunday I thought Martin had not gott my letter on saturday but I see that you found out about it. it is so nice and good and pleasant here its much better than where I was before. it is so nice and evryone is so frendly and kind to me. I am much better now and I get such nice food its so good to eat I eat so much and then I get half a litre of milk to drink every day. I will soon get fat you know. the Chaplin has been here twice it was so nice he is so frendly and kind. I got books from him and I have many other books too I read all the time it is so nice because then I dont remember the children and you so much. it is so sad what I did but if I believe God has forgiven me then it feels better. the Docktor has been here twice he is so frendly and kind I think he said I should be admitted to the Infirmery. he said I can be well again and come back home and have more children it was so nice imagine if I could get well again I think it is a serious illness I have I pray to God that I can be well again ask Farmor to pray for me evry night

we also have a nurse. Sister is so terribly kind and frendly to me sometimes Sister pats me Sister understands how sad and hard it is for me because I did what I done. I get medicine from Sister 3 times a day there are also 5 other Ladies who work here. they are dressed like nurses but there are no more than 3 of them here each day now I am not tired and we also have a little church here it is so lovely I walked through it when I went to see Sister for a blood test and I got weighed. I lie in bed all the time which is good because it is so comftable. But soon I must get up then I will get work to do it will be so nice I feel ready to get up now we get coffee 2 times a day here

I would like you to come here at midsummer because I shall be better then. I would like Holger to bring the car and come too Dagny said in her letter that she thought about coming to see me when I was in Vänersborg but now she thinks it is too far and expensive. I would like her to come and mother as well if she is up to it it would be so nice to see you all once more so please reply to this as soon as you can I am waiting for you come by train otherwise there are 2 sundays then as you know. and now I must end for now Much love to all of you at Haggården love to Evald father and mother Love to Ester and all the little children from me.

Ingeborg
Miss Lindegren wrote the address I am waiting
for a letter say if you are coming by car. come
I hope you can read this I write so ugly

Books and Knitting

The prison bell had just struck one o'clock, and Ingeborg was having dinner in her cell when there was a knock at the door. As usual on Thursdays, she was having pork and peas, with pancakes for dessert.

Ingeborg recognized Dr Goldkuhl's hesitant knock. He visited her at least once a week, but every time it felt as though Ingeborg's life was suddenly paused. The spoon was suspended in mid-air as the hand raising it to her mouth froze, and Ingeborg stopped chewing, sitting there with a wide-open mouth and rosy cheeks.

"Good day to you, Ingeborg, may I come in?" inquired the doctor, who had started addressing her by her first name some time ago. "Don't let me interrupt your dinner."

Ingeborg was ashamed of her voracious appetite, of the way she shovelled in her food. After a month and a half in prison, she had gained four kilograms. She should have left one of the pancakes.

"There will be another day tomorrow," she could hear Mother Selma saying when Dr Goldkuhl patted her on the shoulder and asked if the food was tasty.

"Yes, thank you."

Ingeborg was feeling a little calmer. She no longer spent all her time in bed, but woke up at seven every morning, just like the other inmates. She cleaned her cell and got dressed before breakfast. Perhaps God had not abandoned her after all? Maybe he could forgive her?

"I've brought along a new book today," said Dr Goldkuhl, holding up a copy of *The Silver Rapids* by Elin Wägner.

He wondered whether this book might be too difficult. The books might help Ingeborg to dispel her thoughts, but she had difficulty retaining what she had read. She gave uncertain or incorrect answers about most of the books. She was not even willing to comment on or discuss *The Wonderful Adventure of Nils Holgersson*, which she seemed to have really liked. But she was now able to talk about her family without immediately bursting into tears, so the worst of her anxiety seemed to have dissipated.

"Do you often think about your husband and children?" asked Dr Goldkuhl.

Ingeborg thought about Artur and the children all the time. Although she tried to let it be, she could find no peace. During the day it was easier to keep the thoughts at bay, unless Dr Goldkuhl reminded her, but in the mornings and the evenings they came thick and fast. She was afraid Artur would fall ill, because he had been so fond of the children.

"But what about Mama?" Tor had wondered when Artur had asked him if he wanted to go and try out the new skis he got for Christmas.

"Mama will be fine by herself for a little while, won't you, Ingeborg?" Artur had replied, and Ingeborg nodded.

Tor bundled up all by himself, but Artur helped him lace up his boots, which were too big, so they had to start over after doubling up on the socks. Tor sat down on the hall steps with his left ski resting against the top step, as Artur had taught him. That meant he only had to deal with one leg and one ski at a time. Holding on to the handrail with one hand, he used his other hand to fasten the bindings. Tor tried to stand up, but his right ski had a momentum of its own. His legs and the rest of his body followed, until he managed to steady himself with his ski poles. He glided off across the yard, past the henhouse and down to the road, where Artur was waiting. To bring himself to a halt, he sat down on the ground. His progress came to an abrupt end when Tor ran over Artur's skis, lost his balance and fell head over heels into the blackcurrant bush by the ditch. Ingeborg, who was watching from behind the curtains, rushed to open the window.

"How did it go?" she called, hearing two sets of laughter in reply.

Tor thrashed his arms and legs to create a cloud of snow, while Artur waved his ski pole cheerily before pulling Tor back to his feet.

"Be careful," she whispered to herself, recalling how the process of waxing the skis the previous week had nearly ended in a blaze when Artur had burned in the wood tar over an open fire, almost causing the ski tips to straighten out.

Father and son slithered onward across the road toward the flat strip of field belonging to the neighbour. They made for the boulder in the middle of the pasture, the big rock that

Ingeborg's father had been unable to conquer. The rock had proved too heavy to move and use in a stone wall, and now lay there in isolation like a sandbank in the sea.

Ingeborg didn't want to talk about Artur and the children. She picked up the sock she was knitting in the hope that Dr Goldkuhl would leave soon. He ought to realize she had work to do. The chaplain often said it was important for inmates to work alone during their first year in prison, so that they had time for moral reflection, remorse and insight. Dr Goldkuhl didn't seem to care what the chaplain said. He stayed where he was, making notes.

Ingeborg is skilled at handiwork and works away diligently at her sock knitting. After 2–3 weeks, she is producing near-normal results, he wrote on her chart.

"Tor is cutting strips for rag rugs with his mother, as usual," the nurserymaid had said when Farmor walked into the kitchen and inquired what her grandson was up to.

"Tor is a good lad, helping his mother," Ingeborg had heard Farmor saying. "But do they have to keep working in the parlour? Nobody works in the parlour. You should know that, Artur, even if your wife doesn't know any better."

Ingeborg remembered how she had been startled when Farmor opened the door to show her the covers she had made for the dining chairs to keep the dust off the damask upholstery.

"At the last meeting of the sewing circle at the parsonage, we decided not to hold the auction until November, so you still have more than six months to finish it," Farmor had said, looking at the half-finished rug on the loom. "It was terribly hard to find a suitable date this year," Farmor continued, as she began fitting the new chair covers. "The gravel road can't be freshly graded, because then the girls can't cycle to the auction. And there has to be a full moon so they can see to cycle home safely."

When Tor got up off the creaking floorboards to greet Farmor, she patted him on the head in passing, before continuing her musings on the high and low points of the previous year's needlework auction.

"Nobody bid on my knitted socks last year, you remember, Ingeborg? And your rugs went for way too much! Let's hope the ladies have more sense this year, but they're already lining up to buy your rugs, you know."

The inmates of Växjö Women's Penitentiary sewed towels for the Swedish State Railways and shirts for the army. In Ingeborg's first year at the prison, almost ninety thousand items were produced: thirty thousand towels, ten thousand sheets, nine thousand pillowcases, eleven thousand pairs of socks, a thousand shirts and various other pieces.

The women were paid different rates depending on which prisoner category they belonged to. As well as pay, the category system determined the prisoners' rights and obligations. For their first two months, all prisoners belonged to Category 1, receiving a work bonus of thirty öre per day. They could use this to buy extra food such as sugar, sausage, milk or margarine, since the government did not spend more than thirty-three öre per inmate per day on food.

If a prisoner worked hard and behaved well, she would automatically be promoted to Category 2, where the work bonus was doubled. She was allowed to have a calendar and family photographs in her cell. After two years, she might be promoted to Category 3, which entitled her to a chair with a back, a pocket watch, her own books, and the opportunity to subscribe to various appropriate periodicals. After a year in Category 3, she could decorate her cell as she wished with curtains, flowers on the table and her own handiwork. Small personal belongings such as a powder compact, a pot of rouge, a lipstick or a cigarette case were also allowed, although the superintendent always had custody of the matches.

Who belonged to which category was a matter for the governing committee, which was chaired by the prison governor and the chaplain. Because the categories were constantly changing, it was hard for the prison staff to keep track of each inmate's category, so a small slate in a wooden frame was fitted to each cell door. A red frame indicated Category 1, a green frame Category 2, and a white frame Category 3. The inmate's offence, sentence and category were listed on the slate. The slates faced inward, so that inmates could not see one another's details, but whenever they had the chance they would try to turn over the slates and sneak a look.

"You are being moved to the infirmary at long last, Ingeborg," said Dr Goldkuhl, changing the subject. "That will be a good thing."

Inmates of the infirmary were allocated a large, bright cell, which they could furnish as they liked straight away. They were not confined to their cells, but could work in the day room alongside fellow inmates. And they were allowed to keep their lights on until nine o'clock at night.

"If you remain lucid like this, I shall ask the governor to allow your cell door to stay unlocked," Dr Goldkuhl continued.

Ingeborg nodded.

"In two weeks' time, I should like you to come to my consulting room and answer a few questions. It's nothing to worry about, Ingeborg. Sort of like a homework quiz at school, to find out what you know. Sister Gunhild will come and fetch you and bring you along to my office."

Ingeborg nodded again.

"Did you know, Ingeborg, that my father was also the prison doctor here? He was here for thirty years, just like me. He started in 1872, and I took over when he retired. Thirty years is a long time.

a very long time," said Dr Goldkuhl, looking out of the window. "You haven't even reached thirty yet, Ingeborg."

He suddenly seemed so old and tired. Until now he had never struck Ingeborg as old. His hands were smooth and soft — certainly not working hands. Perhaps the pomade concealed his grey hairs? Or did he dye his hair?

"My father's name was August. August Edward. My son is also called August. We named him after my father. August is the same age as you, by the way. He studied medicine as well. At Lund. We're not very imaginative in our family," said Dr Goldkuhl, attempting a smile. "We are hoping August will stay in Lund. The good people of Växjö need a change, don't you think, Ingeborg?"

Ingeborg continued to stare at the floor, not knowing what to say.

"Were you happy in your marriage, Ingeborg?"

Ingeborg looked up, surprised by the sudden turn the conversation had taken. Then she thought of that day in June of 1923. Ingeborg had stood beside Artur at the altar in the 18th-century triangular chancel, looking out over the congregation. The wedding ceremony had just concluded with the pastor pronouncing them husband and wife. Artur, dressed in a black morning coat and a shiny top hat, had given her such a long kiss that her myrtle crown ended up askew. Ingeborg's eldest sister, there with her husband and their four children, had blushed. They were sitting in the front row of the packed stone church, next to Ingeborg's eldest brother, who was accompanied by his wife and their son Liss, already a teenager. Ivar the pauper was sitting in the back row with Evald, their farmhand.

Ingeborg's four other siblings were also present. Only her father was missing. Although they lived in the heart of western Sweden's bible belt, her father was not particularly religious. He was annoyed by the

Pentecostalists and missionaries, who enticed away more members of the parish by the day, and wondered what the future held for the established church, even though he never attended services himself.

"I would rather think about God as I walk behind my horse than sit in church thinking about the horse," he always said, but that was not why he was absent on Ingeborg's big day. He had taken to his bed again and could no longer get up. Back pain was not the only reason; there was something else wrong with him.

The pastor cleared his throat. The murmur subsided, and the organist took his seat, stepped on the pedals and began playing. He knew his stuff, no doubt about it, but he was getting on a bit and occasionally had trouble keeping time. Matters were not helped by the parishioners, led by the pastor's wife, racing through the hymns as though they were horses running a race. Ingeborg wondered how they were going to make it out of the church before the organist stopped playing. She held on tight to Artur's arm to avoid tripping over her dress. They were greeted by a shower of rice when the verger opened the doors.

"Three cheers and one cheer more for the happy couple!" cried Farmor. "Hip, hip, hooray! Hooray! Hooray! Hooray!"

Ingeborg's long veil trailed on the ground as she descended the steps.

"They were in a hell of a rush to tie the knot," remarked Ivar, spitting into his hand. "It's not long since Artur proposed, so I heard. Maybe they had to?"

"You're just envious, Ivar," Farmor replied. "Now be quiet and go home."

"Well, yes, when we were newly married we were happy," Ingeborg replied

"Aren't we all?" sighed Dr Goldkuhl, looking out of the window. "We are all happy when we're newly married. Then we let life get in the way."

The cows were grazing peacefully in the shade of the trees beyond the fence back home. The crowns of the birch trees were swaying gently in the meadow. Despite the warm morning sunlight, the dew lingered in the small, bright green, newly sprouted leaves on the trees. Ingeborg's father, a stooped man in worn blue overalls, was leaning on a weatherbeaten scythe and gazing out over his fields.

He had been hand-tilling the meagre soil all his life, to the point where he was bent double over his stick. But he had never been able to conquer the big rock on the strip of land bordering the next farm. Not even a crowbar would shift it. The boulder remained stubbornly in place. Isolated, like a skerry surrounded by the sea. The rest of the barren ground, studded with stones and endless mounds of heather, had yielded seven acres of arable land and two hundred metres of stone wall after thirty years of toil.

The stone wall with its silvery lichen encircled the churchyard like a symbolic boundary between clergy and peasants. A monument to poverty and to a place cursed by God, where the land was a mixture of hard, stony, tussocked soil and boggy tracts of sedge and moss.

Ingeborg's father, a lean man, bent forward to snip off a couple of withered violets in his garden patch. The spring tillage and the sowing were done, and now he was concerned about the mood of the weather gods. After a winter with little snow, a dry spell in the early summer would not be good. Unable to enjoy the quiet period before the harvest, he allowed his anxiety about the hay to cloud out the warm rays of the sun.

"I had a good life," said Ingeborg eventually, without meeting Dr Goldkuhl's eyes.

"Can't you look up sometimes when we're talking to each other, Ingeborg?"

It sounded so brusque. Harsh and impatient. That was not the doctor's intention, but for a moment he forgot he was at work. He forgot that he was not at home talking to his wife. He forgot to conceal his anger, his unease, his frustration. How could his wife do this to him? As if it were her fault that she was ill. As if it were anyone's fault. He was a doctor. His father was a doctor. His son was a doctor. God almighty, his whole family were doctors! A family of doctors. And no-one, no-one could do anything.

Ingeborg looked up for a moment, as if obeying an order. Then she did not move a muscle until he had left the cell.

Next time, Dr Goldkuhl decided, he would stick to questions about the family and practical matters. Ingeborg's family. He had let his professionalism slip today, allowing his own concerns and his fears for his wife's health to get the better of him. Perhaps he was unnecessarily worried? Maybe it wasn't too serious?

Monday May 27th.

My Dear Little Artur

Dear Artur I am now waiting for a letter did you not get my letter or are you too busy with the springtime to write it is so nice to get a letter from you. I am so happy because I am so well and also I dont remember the children so much now since I got midicine it is so nice. I am sleeping so well and eating just as well. I weighed myself this week now I weigh 57 kilos when I came here I weigh 53 kilos Docktor Goldkhus was here this week he said I can get up soon. it is so nice to lie down I think I got 3 big Candies from him, he ask if I like candies the Chaplin was also here this week it is so nice when he comes. I can now go to Church every sunday I started going on Assension Day at Whitsun I was there both days on Whitsun Eve I was knitting socks it is so nice I knit one sock a day, I get 15 öre for a pair more when I get up then I can weave ribbons and I can also go out every day it will be so nice. Miss Appelgren comes every monday and we discus if we need to buy anything there is everything here we get what we want to buy I buy a half kilo apples it cost 75 öre but on Saturday I bought a jar of herring it was so good with a sanwich it cost 50 öre I shall buy it instead of apples in dill sauce every other week also I bought 4 buns them cost 10 öre we can buy cookies too I am really looking fourward to you coming here at Midsummer. The Docktor said you should not come more than one or two at a time he said I am not so strong yet. I wrote to Karin at Witsun and to Mother on Sunday I wrote that I would like Dagny and Tali to come here if they dont think it cost too much my tickit here from Vänersborg cost 50 if I remember right but the Superintendent said it is not so far for you via Borås then you only have to change at Borås and Alvesta it will be so nice when you come write soon and tell me if you are coming then I wont have to wait so much. Write soon now you must be busy with the spring Mrs Tor said that spring is over here already, I have such a nice room I have a table 1 chair 1 bed a washstand 1 mirror 1 comb 1 soap 1 vase of Birch Leaves the leaves are so green and lovely here 1 vase of flowers a tree I got from Sister it has so many flowers it is so beautyful Sister is so kind and Sweet I think if you knew that you would be so happy all of them are so kind to me. it is so nice I like it so much here I get up at 7 a.m. and go to sleep at half past 7 p.m. now I am out of monney so I would like you to send me 10 kronor strait away.

send it to me in a letter by registered mail please I had 650 when I came here tell me about when you buried the little children and who was there when you done it who carried the little children to the church yard are those little children resting in the same place as grandfather tell me when you write back Much love to all of you at Haggården. Ingeborg.

Violets

"Please take a seat," said Dr Goldkuhl when his patient appeared.

Sister Gunhild, who had accompanied Ingeborg to the consulting room, stayed to exchange a few words with the doctor. Meanwhile, Ingeborg stood motionless by the door, her hands folded and her head bowed. She had a tendency to freeze in such uncomfortable positions and an apparent ability to stand like that for an unlimited time. When at work, however, she often moved with unwarranted, almost impetuous haste.

"Aren't you getting tired standing up, Ingeborg?" inquired Dr Goldkuhl once Sister Gunhild had left, repeating his invitation to sit down.

Ingeborg made no reply, but sat down with her head bowed and began picking at her hands. Initially Dr Goldkuhl had put this down to shyness, but as he had got to know the young woman, he started to think her behaviour was in no small measure stereotypical. For instance, if she had to exert herself, she showed slight contractions in her facial muscles. He asked if she had always had the same patterns of movement — if she often sat or stood still without realizing it, or forgot what she was doing.

"Farmor sometimes used to say I should be able to do more than I did," she answered quietly. "And Tor sometimes asked why I wasn't doing anything."

"Did your husband ever complain about it?"

"Artur always did as I asked."

Ingeborg had asked her husband if they could go to the Jubilee Exhibition in Gothenburg in the spring of 1923, and Artur had not taken much persuading. His brother had driven them to Ljung station. The train journey had gone smoothly, but the cable car ride up to Liseberg almost ended in disaster. They had stood in line at Näckrosdammen for more than an hour to get on board, and were crowded into one of the cars along with ten other passengers when the vehicle came to a sudden stop and began to sway. Artur, who was afraid of heights, scarcely dared look down at the historical pageant passing beneath them on Södra vägen, but Ingeborg counted sixteen floats: heralds dressed in blue and white, Stone Age people from the coastal meadows, Bronze Age inhabitants of Bohuslän, East India Company merchants carrying blue porcelain and yellow silk from China. The entire population of the city through the ages was depicted.

After a while, a couple of students became impatient and clambered down the emergency escape line. They landed on the float portraying a whale in the ocean next to a Viking dragon ship. The peasant clearing his turnip patch beside them cried out, thinking Judgment Day was at hand. Eventually the car operator got the machinery started again, and Artur calmed down after having a bite to eat. Then they had taken a spin round the dance floor at the Rotunda.

"What an adventure you've brought me on, Artur!" Ingeborg exclaimed.

"We'll have to come back when we have a family," Artur replied, pointing out the Children's Paradise.

But Ingeborg had already spied the gaudy postcards on sale at the kiosk opposite and was getting her purse out of her handbag. She bought two cards and a ten-öre stamp. She mailed one of the cards to her sister and kept the other as a souvenir.

"Just think what I've been missing out on back here in the village!" she had said when they got home, putting the card in one of the wooden frames that Holger had carved for them as a wedding present. "Now I want to see all the cities in Sweden!"

"We must take the opportunity before the children come along," Artur had replied, but it was not to be.

She was already pregnant with Tor.

"Do you love your husband?" asked the doctor.

"I always got my way," answered Ingeborg. "And no matter how tired he was, he was never mean to the children. He even read them stories at night."

"Were you ever unkind to your children, Ingeborg?"

She pinched them sometimes, so she did, when they were too rambunctious. But most of the time the boys behaved themselves, and she always feared they were going to die when they were sick.

Efraim had arrived barely two years after Tor. They had baptized him at home during the moose hunt. A hush fell over the family, but Efraim had cried throughout the ceremony. Efraim was always crying, but the pastor was unfazed. He had taken out his Bible and turned to chapter eighteen of St Luke's Gospel.

Suffer little children to come unto me, and forbid them not: for of such is the kingdom of God.

She remembered how she had stood in front of the parlour window, pale, with dark circles under her eyes, holding the screaming bundle of fine white tulle in her arms. Artur stood next to her at the high table that was serving as a makeshift altar. Mother Selma had placed a thick christening candle on Farmor's hand-stitched Hardanger doily. The flame flickered in the draught, even though the inner panes of the windows had been in place since the autumn equinox and the insulation batts were sitting snugly between the panes. Tor sat on the floor at her feet, sucking on the edge of her long black skirt. Dressed for the occasion in a blue and white striped sailor suit, he would be two years old at Easter.

"Efraim, I baptize you in the name of the Father and of the Son and of the Holy Ghost," the pastor continued, pouring the water of life over the child's bald head.

Elsa had assumed her position at the piano, her back straight and her hands resting in her lap. Since the U.S. Congress had passed new, stricter immigration laws, she had been unable to return to her job at the post office in Chicago. Her uncle had helped her file an appeal against the decision, but apparently the authorities could take months to respond. She received lengthy letters every week, and the occasional parcel, from her fiancé, a newly rich farmer from Oregon whom she had met at night school.

"Almighty God, Thou alone can save us from all evil. Deliver Efraim from the power of darkness, write his name in the Book of Life, and keep him in Thy light now and for evermore. Amen. And now let us welcome this child into our congregation by singing the first three verses of hymn number 248," said the pastor in conclusion.

When Elsa placed her fingers on the keys and began playing the introduction to *Children of the Heavenly Father*, Ingeborg went into the bedroom to feed her younger son. She sat in the rocking chair, and Efraim quietened down for a moment. She closed her eyes, dreaming of days gone by, and fell asleep. A few minutes later, her mother opened the door without knocking first.

"You can't be sitting out here in the dark by yourself on a big day like this," said Selma. "Come out and behave like a proper person, then we won't need to feel ashamed."

When Ingeborg opened her eyes, Selma had already turned on her heels and left the room to rejoin the others. She laid Efraim in the cradle that Artur had built in the evenings during their first winter together. On the short side, he had etched the names of the two boys. She threw the sheepskin blanket over the boy to keep him warm and stroked his brown hair gently. He was such a nice, calm child when asleep.

"It was a nice thought, naming the boy after his grandfather," said Farmor, entering the room and patting her daughter-in-law on the shoulder. "May he rest in peace."

Together they returned to the parlour, where Dagny, Ingeborg's sister, had started serving coffee and cake.

"The child isn't sick, is he?" asked Selma when her daughter had pulled up a chair and sat down at the table. "Or why didn't you have the christening in church like everyone else?"

"It's deathly cold out there," replied Liss, whose voice had just broken.

"Anyone can see there is something up with him. Anyway, I've bought him an engraved silver spoon as a christening gift, to be on the safe side," said Selma. "I shall place it in his cradle tonight to ward off the evil one."

"Mother, stop spreading superstitions and old wives' tales," said Dagny.

"You didn't invite your fiancé, then, Dagny?" inquired Artur.

Ingeborg's sister blushed, and when she hesitated in answering, Farmor stepped in to support her.

"They've only just met, Artur. Don't be so nosy!"

"That doesn't matter! She's lived with us for more than two years now, and I want her to feel at home," said Artur. "You've bagged yourself a damn good shot, by the way," he went on, turning to Dagny.

"Don't swear," whispered Ingeborg. "What if the pastor heard you?"

"Her fellow brought down a yearling on yesterday's hunt, so we can look forward to venison on Sunday," said Artur, ignoring Ingeborg's reprimand.

"Delicious!" said Dagny quietly, with a smile.

"Yes, you never would have thought that the hunting club's training in the rutting sounds of moose bulls would pay off so quickly," said Artur.

"Be careful," said Ingeborg. "You know what Mother always says about those wretched dance halls."

Dagny nodded and blushed even more deeply. To spare her further embarrassment, Liss changed the subject.

"When are we going to have a beer to wet the baby's head?"

"Beer? Not until you're dry behind the ears, boy!" said Artur with a laugh. "Although perhaps Mother Selma would like a cognac for the road?"

"No need. You'll stay for the evening, won't you, Mother?" said Ingeborg.

"Yes, perhaps you'd even like to stay over?" suggested Farmor.

"Yes, Farmor and Selma can sleep top and tail in the cottage."

"I don't know what has got into my son today," said Farmor, shaking her head. "Please excuse him. He is just so happy and proud of his two boys. But there will be no need for sleeping top and tail. Surely you can make up a bed on the kitchen sofa for your mother, Ingeborg, so that she doesn't have to venture out in this dreadful winter weather?"

"I alone am responsible for the death of the children," said Ingeborg eventually. "I understand the severity of the crime I have committed."

"What happened, Ingeborg, happened because you were ill," said Dr Goldkuhl.

"I don't know that."

"Had you ever acted impulsively like that before?"

"Farmor thought I was flighty," said Ingeborg, looking down at her hands in her lap.

She rubbed her hands together and fixed her gaze on the bunch of flowers on the desk, noticing the purple-blue petals and the heart-shaped leaves. When she was a child, she used to pick violets with her mother on the hillside leading down to the river. Dr Goldkuhl's flowers reminded her of the early summer days of her childhood. They smelled like the glade on the edge of the woods after a night of rain, the glade back home next to the cow pasture.

"Do you like violets, Ingeborg?"

Ingeborg was startled, as if Dr Goldkuhl had caught her up to some mischief. She made no answer, but the doctor paid no heed to her lack of response. He too was lost in thought, thinking about his sick wife at home as he flicked through the transcripts of Ingeborg's police interviews. Her psychiatric examination was scheduled for

June 30, 1929. That was only a few days away, so he had to bring up the difficult questions.

"You told me, Ingeborg, that you were going to clean the kitchen after doing the laundry and then bake wheat buns in the afternoon that day," he began. "Your husband was president of the rifle club, and they were going to have a meeting at your home the next day. Were you afraid the buns were not going to turn out well?"

"Artur's brother was the treasurer," said Ingeborg.

"I beg your pardon?"

"My brother-in-law was treasurer of the rifle club."

"Yes, that's correct, he was treasurer. Were you overwhelmed by the responsibility of baking the buns?"

"No."

"Why did you take the lives of the children?"

"I was not thinking anything. If I had been thinking, I would not have done so."

"How did you feel afterwards, Ingeborg?"

"Empty."

"Were you not affected by the dismay of those around you, the questions they asked, the emotions they expressed?"

"No."

"Were you not affected by your arrest and the long journey to Vänersborg?"

"I quickly fell asleep. I slept well and had no dreams on my first night in jail."

"Do you often think about the children?"

"I feel sorry for the children. But they are probably fine now. They are with God."

Ingeborg looked at the bunch of flowers on Dr Goldkuhl's desk. The doctor followed her gaze, and just then there was a knock at the door.

"Here comes Sister Gunhild, that's good," he said, getting up. "We were just finishing."

The doctor waved somewhat awkwardly, with his right hand hanging by his side — as though he had intended to extend it but had suddenly remembered that was not a good idea because Ingeborg never shook hands. Too often he had been left standing there with his hand in mid-air, not knowing what to do with it.

"See you again soon, Ingeborg. Would you like to take the violets back to your room?" he continued, picking up the glass vase as Ingeborg made her way out of the door.

"But, but..."

"Yes, yes, I know. The rules," sighed Dr Goldkuhl, waving his free hand dismissively. "Don't worry about the rules today, Ingeborg. I shall take responsibility for the flowers."

"You're so kind, Dr Goldkuhl. The Good Lord will reward you one day," said Sister Gunhild, hurrying over to the doctor to accept the gift. "I'll bring the flowers along to your room, Mrs Andersson," she continued, sticking her nose into the mass of blue petals. "They smell so lovely."

"Ingeborg, do you realize that you have been very ill?" asked Dr Goldkuhl seriously as Sister Gunhild disappeared into the corridor.

The doctor took a step forward and tried to make eye contact with his patient, but Ingeborg, who had briefly looked up at the violets, was staring down at the floor again.

"I did it myself," she mumbled.

"Yes, I know. You said so. But did you really not hear any voices?" persisted Dr Goldkuhl, taking Ingeborg's hands in his.

"No," replied Ingeborg firmly, pulling herself free. "I am prepared to go to prison for life."

Dear Mr Andersson,

The doctor asked me to write you this short note asking you kindly not to forget your wife. She is such a lovable, sweet person. As you will understand, she has been ill, and it is partly your fault that this happened. You saw her every day and must have noticed that she was not quite well, so she is not solely to blame for everything. Please treat her now in a spirit of forgiveness and compassion, which she needs so much, as she is so sorely troubled by everything. But she has great love for Artur, whom she is always thinking about and waiting for. Do not forget her, as everything can become brighter for both of you. Sometimes, even the darkest and most difficult things can have some meaning, although we never comprehend it here on Earth. Please write her a letter and, if possible, come and visit her, as she is so lonely. Forgive me, but I badly want to make things right again. Ingeborg needs help. We are all so fond of her; she is a good little soul, and everything she did was a result of her illness. Hope to hear from you soon.

With sympathy,
Gunhild Larsson
Nursing Sister

NATIONAL BOARD OF CORRECTIONS

Name Day

"Happy name day, Mrs Andersson!" said Sister Gunhild, opening the door to Ingeborg's cell and placing a vase on the table.

"What gorgeous flowers!" exclaimed Ingeborg, taking a sniff of the delicately formed, white, bell-like blooms and stroking the shiny, pointed leaves. "I used to sell lilies of the valley at the market in Borås when I was little."

"Is that so?" said Sister Gunhild, nodding in the direction of Ingeborg's hymn book. "I see you are getting close to the end. Has your systematic reading paid off yet?"

Ingeborg flicked back about a dozen pages. The brittle paper almost disintegrated as she eagerly showed the nurse a well-thumbed page.

"I think so," she whispered, pointing to the second verse on the page:

> In sooth 'tis not the mind of God,
> His anger ever endeth,

> Return we, He removes the rod,
> And to the weary sendeth
> A sweet release,
> To mark doth cease,
> And visit our transgressing;
> His wrath He turns,
> And tow'rd us yearns,
> Gives after cursing blessing.³

"So beautiful. So true. I'm glad you came across that and are finding comfort in the word of God," said Sister Gunhild when she had finished reading.

"Were there no letters for me again today?"

"No, not today," replied Sister Gunhild, placing her hand on Ingeborg's. "But wait and see, you'll surely hear from him soon."

"I think Artur has forgotten all about me."

"Don't say that, Mrs Andersson. You must not lose heart. There is a meaning to everything. The ways of the Lord are unfathomable."

"Poor Artur! It would have been better if I had died. Then the little children would still be alive."

Ingeborg felt the nausea welling up. Her breathing became laboured, and she had to swallow hard.

Farmers and crofters, maids and farmhands, the young and the aged — the entire population of the village, summoned by the bells, had flocked to God's house that Sunday morning in the summer of 1927. They crowded into the newly built vestibule, pushing forward to find a vacant seat, anxious to rest their weary feet or to doze off to the sound of the Whitsun hymns or the pastor's sermon on how the Holy Ghost revealed itself to Jerusalem's apostles.

Ingeborg hurried outside for a breath of air. It was muggy, and dark clouds were looming on the horizon. She crept behind the bell tower and sobbed. Hunched over in her light brown dress and grey pinafore, she looked like a little sparrow after the autumn moulting. Artur had tried to follow her, but three-year-old Tor refused to let go of his father's hand, and on his other arm Artur was holding the sleeping Efraim.

After a while, Ingeborg returned with relief to the church and caught up with her family in the middle of the aisle. The front rows were reserved for the families of landowners and the clergy. Tor continued to fret.

"Buddy, you just need to let go of my hand for a moment so I can open the door of the pew," explained Artur.

Ivar the pauper came to the rescue, and Artur nodded gratefully. Tor jumped up into the pew contentedly, and Artur smiled at his eldest son, whose legs were dangling from his short trousers. His new shoes were thumping softly against the back of the pew in front, and Artur shushed him.

"Boys will be boys," said Ivar good-naturedly, shaking his bald head. "You can sit here, Ingeborg," he went on, getting to his feet and indicating the spot where he had been sitting.

"No need for you to stand, Ivar. There's room for all of us," said Artur, lifting Tor onto his lap and squeezing up a little closer. "You look awfully pale," he continued, turning to Ingeborg as she sat down beside him. "Perhaps you should have stayed at home to rest today. We can look after ourselves for a couple of hours, can't we, boys?"

"For sure," replied Tor precociously.

Artur was rummaging in his trouser pocket for something. Efraim awoke and looked up inquisitively from Artur's shoulder.

"Here you go," said Artur, handing Ingeborg a cough drop. "Suck on this and you'll soon feel better. "You probably didn't have enough to eat this morning, I bet."

"Can we try them too?" asked Tor, lighting up when Artur handed him the whole cone of candies and told him to share the rest with his brother.

"Let's go for a walk," said Sister Gunhild, taking down the hanger with the heavy homespun vest from its hook on the wall.

Ingeborg took it and opened the fastenings. The burlap lining was prickly, even though she was wearing the grey, blue and black cotton chequered dress underneath.

"I can never escape what I have done."

"You must not forget that you were ill, Mrs Andersson," said Sister Gunhild. "You have been sorely tested by God and given a heavy cross to bear. Who are you to judge and to add yet more stones to your burden?"

It was three o'clock when they stepped out into the exercise yard, a miniature panopticon resembling an open fan, divided into nine segments by high wooden boards. At the centre point of the fan, from the tall watchtower, the superintendent kept an eye on the prisoners walking back and forth within the confines of their respective segments. From above, the segments resembled slices of pie. In the centre of the semicircle, in front of the doorway, someone had planted a flowerbed.

"Take a walk in the garden instead," called the superintendent, waving from the watchtower. "It's Mrs Andersson's name day, after all!"

"Yes, let's do as the superintendent suggests, but all of you must promise me that you'll ignore any invitations from the brewers."

Sister Gunhild looked knowingly at a twenty-four-year-old strumpet from Västergötland, who was doing time for prostitution but had learned to read and write in prison. When her little girl was trampled to death by a runaway horse on her way home from school, the strumpet had started writing love poems, and Sister Gunhild believed it was only a matter of time before she would find peace with the Lord. The chaplain was not so sure.

"With an old witch for a mother, who believes in ghosts that talk drivel, it could hardly have ended in anything but prostitution," he said.

Shortly after, the stench of mash from the vats hit them as they approached the imposing building painted in yellow and red ochre. The Kristineberg Brewery, which employed thirty men, was located on a hill in the northeast corner of the prison gardens. One of the workers whistled and threw a couple of bottles of beer over the wall while Sister Gunhild wasn't looking. He could barely be heard above the clatter of bottles from the plant. The strumpet giggled and quickly hid both bottles inside her dress.

"What a way to behave!" exclaimed old Emma, who nevertheless distracted Sister Gunhild so that she wouldn't go telling tales to the chaplain.

As the women were heading back to the prison, Sister Gunhild took Ingeborg's arm and asked her quietly:

"How about throwing a party on your birthday, Mrs Andersson? Like the strumpet did when you first arrived. The girls would probably enjoy that."

Funny Questions

"Did you sleep well, Ingeborg?" inquired Dr Goldkuhl, writing the date in the top right corner of the oral intelligence test, after Sister Gunhild had brought Ingeborg to his office on the morning of June 30, 1929.

"I am now going to run through ten pages of standard questions. It will take quite a while, but please don't fret. Just try to do your best, Ingeborg."

The purpose of the psychiatric examination was to assess patients' grounding in reality and their conformity to social norms, and to test their understanding of religion, history and geography and their general knowledge.

The exercises included interpreting proverbs, critically examining apparent illogicalities, and answering questions on abstract and ethical concepts. This was in order to assess patients' character, interpersonal skills and degree of socialization. The test did not result in a grade and was intended solely as a guide for the examining physician.

"So, Ingeborg, I should like you to begin by reading this fable to me," said Dr Goldkuhl.

Ingeborg read the tale of the dog and the bone without once stumbling over her words. She was good at reading from the page, and no-one could dispute that. When Dr Goldkuhl asked her to recount the content of the story after she had finished reading, she omitted only a few minor details. She did well with the fable of the lion and the mouse too. The tales were illustrated, and Ingeborg described both pictures correctly, but at times her descriptions went beyond what was shown in the images.

"Can we really see the dog gaping at the bone in the water and, in so doing, losing his own bone?" asked Dr Goldkuhl.

"No, but it says so," replied Ingeborg.

The letter-writing exercise did not go so well. Ingeborg didn't know what to write about and spent too long pondering, becoming stressed and nervous. She began describing the pullout sofa bed in the kitchen back home, and how she and her big sister would use the lid as a slide when they were little, but she ran short of time and was unsure of how to spell some of the words.

Twenty-five years later, Ingeborg had hissed at Tor and Efraim to calm down when they had played the same game.

"Come on, let's play ride a cock-horse instead," said Dagny, extending her hand to Tor.

Tor ran straight over and sat on his aunt's leg, reciting the nursery rhyme as he bounced up and down. Efraim, who had been sitting on Dagny's lap but had now crawled down to the floor, tried to clamber up her other leg.

"No, hold on!" said Dagny with a laugh. "I'm not *that* strong, you know."

Ingeborg was standing at the stove boiling diapers. That was when she had announced that she was pregnant again, in her third month with Lucia.

"Me too!" her sister had said, and started crying.

"What are you saying? Have you told Mother and Father?" Ingeborg had asked.

"Not yet. I couldn't bring myself to tell them," replied Dagny. "But I shall have to do it soon. I'm going to start showing any day now."

"What are you going to do?"

"He has proposed," said Dagny, wiping away her tears. "He's not as well off as Artur, but he is kind."

"I don't know how I'm going to manage without you," said Ingeborg.

"What, has someone died?" inquired Liss when he and Artur returned from the woods. "You two look awful grave."

"Dagny is moving away to get married," replied Ingeborg.

"Why, that's great news!" exclaimed Artur. "Warmest congratulations! You've found yourself a fine fellow."

The content is confined to a very narrow sphere of interest, the handwriting is childish, and the spelling poor. The content is admittedly lucid, and the sentence structure fairly good, but the punctuation is practically non-existent, noted Dr Goldkuhl, asking Ingeborg to recite the alphabet.

In her haste, Ingeborg forgot the letters u, x and y. She did better at the dictation exercise, writing the numbers 129, 598 and 1,973,817 without difficulty.

The mental arithmetic exercise consisted of forty questions, ten for each of the basic operations. Dr Goldkuhl had to repeat five of the questions, but after a good amount of thinking time, Ingeborg got almost all of them right. She was flushed from the mental exertion and was breathing so heavily that Dr Goldkuhl decided she needed a break.

On the subject of religion, Ingeborg answered half of the eleven questions correctly. She knew the Lord's Prayer by heart, but didn't know which faith she belonged to and could not name any faiths other than Lutheran and Roman Catholic. She knew when and why we celebrate Christmas, but didn't know who Moses and Luther were.

Ingeborg had been sitting by the kitchen window watching a sparrow picking seeds out of a pine cone. Baby Lucia, only two weeks old, was sleeping in her arms. Artur and Ingeborg had named their daughter after the saint's day on which she was born. The nurserymaid put the last plate of saffron buns in the oven and brushed off the baking tray. When Artur arrived home, she went into her room to change, with Efraim toddling along behind.

Artur walked over to the stove and threw a block of wood on the embers. Sparks flew from the white birch bark as the flames took hold of the log. He stretched out his leg toward the open soot door and wiggled his bare toes in front of the fire to regain sensation in his foot. He said it tingled in the heat and started to throb as the blood rushed into the veins. Artur put his foot back down and pulled the sleeve of his sweater over his hand so as not to burn his fingers when emptying the ash pan.

"What do you think, Tor, shall we go for a spin on the skis before it gets dark?" he asked his eldest son when the nurserymaid returned with Efraim on her arm. "It's been snowing all day, so it will be good going."

"That will be fun, won't it, Tor?" said the nurserymaid, turning to the boy, who was sitting on the floor at his mother's feet cutting Artur's old dungarees into strips for rag rugs.

The nurserymaid had put on a long pencil skirt in linen and a dark ruched blouse with covered buttons and white cuffs. A wide, hand-embroidered collar, held in place with a white rosette, covered her broad shoulders.

"Going out on the razzle, I see," said Artur to the nineteen-year-old girl, who was wearing her freshly curled hair in a bun.

"Yes, Liss is coming to pick me up in an hour's time. Some of the local boys are playing their accordions in the village hall tonight."

"So you can stay at home for once, Artur," said Ingeborg.

"I don't mind keeping an eye on the children until Tor and your husband are back," said the nurserymaid to Ingeborg, receiving no answer.

"That's kind of you," said Artur, taking a coin out of his pocket. "Here's a little something extra for taking such good care of the children. Ingeborg is so wrapped up in her weaving, so I know you're left to look after them and the housekeeping on your own."

"How many continents are there?" continued Dr Goldkuhl.

"One."

"How many?" repeated Dr Goldkuhl, surprised.

"I don't know."

"What is the name of the continent you are thinking of, Ingeborg?"

"Europe."

"You can name another continent, can't you?"

"America."

The rest of the eighteen questions on geography related to the southern regions of Sweden, and Ingeborg got almost all of them right. She knew where she was now and where she was born. She knew the name of Sweden's capital city and the population of Stockholm.

The thirty general knowledge questions on the calendar, weights and measures, points of the compass, time and temperature also went well. The only thing Ingeborg forgot was the direction in which the sun rose and set.

She did not fare so well with the history questions, getting only thirteen out of eighteen right. She knew the names of the entire Swedish royal family, and when King Gustav Vasa had lived, but didn't know what a crown prince was. She knew which countries had fought in the world war, but could not remember when it had ended.

Ingeborg easily identified the collective terms 'birds', 'flowers' and 'wild animals', but was at a loss when it came to 'vehicles'.

"Steamships, sailboats, trains, airplanes and automobiles are all machines," she answered.

In a sense that is correct, thought Dr Goldkuhl.

They had been sitting at the kitchen table back home, and Artur had suggested that Liss should take the nurserymaid over to Mellomtorp, where they now had a wireless set.

"Wireless!?" cried Farmor. "What nonsense is this? How can the Rolanders afford these newfangled contraptions? Those crofters would be better off feeding their children a square meal. But he always has to be one up, that fellow at Mellomtorp. First wireless in the village, I'll wager."

"He's proud as a peacock. Got it from his son, who's an electrician in Gothenburg," replied Artur. "Have you bathed your wound, by the way?"

"It's nothing to worry about," said Liss.

"What wound is that?" inquired the nurserymaid, putting the pot of potatoes and a tub of butter on the table. "Dinner is served. Please help yourselves."

"I slipped and cut myself on the pitchfork when we were loading manure," said Liss, pulling up his sweater with his left hand.

The muscles in his right arm were reluctant to comply, and the hand hung limply beside his wiry body. Liss tried to appear unconcerned, but grimaced when the nurserymaid helped him pull away the fabric that had stuck to the dried blood. The pitchfork had torn a long, deep wound in his right side. The skin below the ribs was already turning blue.

"That looks nasty, Liss," said Farmor gravely. "Let me bathe it for you, so you don't end up with blood poisoning."

Dr Goldkuhl carried on with his questions: "What is the difference between a table and a chair?"

"You can't sit on a table," replied Ingeborg.

"Well, yes, but you could sit here if you wanted to, couldn't you?" said the doctor, tapping the desk in front of him.

"No."

"Would it be completely impossible?" asked Dr Goldkuhl, unable to suppress a smile.

"Tables are not made for sitting on."

Dr Goldkuhl gave up and wrote down Ingeborg's answer.

"And now, Ingeborg, I should like you to interpret some proverbs. What is meant by 'fine words butter no parsnips'?"

"Mankind," replied Ingeborg.

Thinking Ingeborg had misunderstood the question, Dr Goldkuhl repeated the saying. On receiving the same answer, he looked up at his patient. Ingeborg realized she had answered incorrectly, pursed her lips and remained silent. In spite of the doctor's explanations, encouragement and persistence, she said nothing. Dr Goldkuhl decided to try another proverb.

"Are you familiar with the saying 'the apple never falls far from the tree'?"

"Yes."

"Do you know what it means?"

"It means mankind."

"How about 'the best-laid schemes of mice and men gang aft agley'?"

"Mankind."

Dr Goldkuhl then went through twelve abstract concepts such as kindness, gratitude, honesty, helpfulness, envy, greed, waste and wickedness, and asked what they meant. Ingeborg was unable to explain the nouns and merely repeated the same word in its adjectival or verbal form.

"Kindness is when people are kind. Waste is when someone wastes all kinds of things. Helpfulness is when one person helps another."

"What does vanity mean?"

"Sin."

"Why must we not steal?"

"It's a sin."

"Why are people punished for committing a crime?"

"Because it's a sin."

"What is the difference between thrift and greed?"

"Thrift is a virtue."

"What are our duties to our parents?"

"To serve them, obey them, love them and cherish them."

Ingeborg knew her catechism by heart. It had been drilled into her and her classmates by Miss Brandberg at Vesene village school. She also gave correct answers to all the practical questions about home and housekeeping.

"That's all," said Dr Goldkuhl in conclusion. "I can tell that you grew up on a farm, Ingeborg. I don't think I could have answered where the best place is to grow potatoes or what a kilogram of butter costs," he added with a smile. "Mind you, I do know the four types of cereal. How are you feeling now?"

"There will be a punishment."

Dr Goldkuhl at once became serious and was lost for words. He had imagined Ingeborg would share his relief that the examination was finally over. He had believed, too, that he had got to know her by this stage. Slightly, at least. But Ingeborg was living in a world of her own. She still did not seem to understand the point of the examination she had just undergone. She had no clear idea of the prison doctor's role in the whole process. His role. It was his letter to the National Board of Medicine that would provide the basis for the board's decision. In spite of all his efforts and everything he had said about her prospects during their conversations over the course of the spring, it all seemed to be completely lost on his patient.

"You were not in full command of your senses when it happened, Ingeborg. You have been very ill and are in need of care."

"Going unpunished is out of the question, since I am so well now," continued Ingeborg. "In another life I hope to go unpunished."

"You have done your best, Ingeborg, and no-one can do more than that," replied Dr Goldkuhl. "I am now going to send off the paperwork to the National Board of Medicine, along with my recommendation, and hope for a response within a couple of months."

"The National Board of Medicine will decide the punishment," said Ingeborg. "I am no longer mentally ill, because I can remember so clearly now."

In his letter to the National Board of Medicine, Dr Goldkuhl wrote:

The patient, who on her father's side has a hereditary predisposition to mental illness, is quiet and reserved by nature. Although she never had an especially robust constitution, she previously always enjoyed good health and presented as happy, industrious and engaged. Entering her 27th year, following two childbirths in fairly short order and the shock of a sudden death in the family, she began to sleep poorly, became taciturn, withdrawn, disengaged, forgetful, was unable to perform her domestic duties as before, became morose and self-accusatory, lost her appetite and lost weight. After this had been going on for about a year, she committed an act entirely at odds with her natural interests and previous disposition, which lacked any motive and was decidedly impulsive in every respect. Immediately thereafter, her emotional side became completely dead. She has since become even more silent and reserved than before and is displaying partial amnesia. She gradually brightens up enough that she can feel remorse and be reasoned with, but still exhibits, at the time of writing, catatonic and demented traits. The diagnosis should not be anything other than catatonic schizophrenia with depressive episodes.

Växjö Sunday June 30th 1929

My Dear little Artur
I wanted to write a few lines to ask if you got my letters or not because you nevver write I sentt a card at Midsummer I have been waiting 2 months for a letter but now I feel really sadd because I dont think you are well I am so affraid you will get sick I remmember so well what you said when I had to leave. then I thought you were so smal and thin hope you are well perhaps have you have so much to do that you dont get around to writing I thinkt about you

all the time write soon and tell me about it you are so teribly and Truely kind I am now so well so you do not need to worry about me Everyone is so kind and frendly to me I can not describe it now I get to stay up all day it is so nice here If only you knew and I get to go out 1 and half hour in the morning and a half in the afternoon now I am weaving ribons it is so nice I get 4 öre per meter and I also can now be in the auxilliary and then I think I will get 70 öre a week I dont know yet then we are in the day room every day we are 9 in all but 4 are confined to bed 2 have gone away and 2 have come Signe age 17 and Elin 41 are from skåne Albertina 40 and Ester 30 from blekinge them confined to bed Hanna 24 and me 28 from Västgöttland Ellen 30 from Smålland Emma 50 from Dalarna the others from Mallmö 2 them confined

I have only been up all day for a week I was only allowed to be up for a half hour a day to begin with it is so nice here on sunday I go to Church from half past 11 till $^1/_2$ past 12. Then we have prayers in the church from 7 in the evening till half past tuesday and thursday 2 days a week Pastor Viding is the Governor now so we have another chaplin Pastor Samuelsson the Governor is on holyday now the Chaplin comes to see us once a week and we get books once a fortnight to read he has a libary. I was so shure you would come at Midsummer when you didnt write it would of been so nice to see you again but now I am so terribly sad when you dont write didnt Holger and Farmor get cards from me I was so shure I would get a letter on my birthday June 14th but you have probably forgotten all about me on June 14th I got a letter from Karin with 10 kronor from Father and Mother I got them on the 13th so then I bought cookies for 172 and 29 öre candies and invited my fellow innmates to coffee on my birthday like Hanna did when it was her birthday that was April 20th when I arrived here them thought it was so good there were 4 kinds of cakes the Nurses deccorated around my coffee cup so beautifully with flowers and leaves. them are no older than between 20 and 30 them are always so happy when we go outside then there are always 2 Gards with us usually them called Mrs Tor Mrs Strandberg Miss Petterson Andersson Lindegren Appelgren Sister Gundhild always come to say good night Sister is so kind and sweet.

at Väneborg the Docktor always came once a week and when I come here the doctor always came once a week when I was sick in bed and then when I start to get upp I had to go to see him for examination I have been in to see him 10 times today was the last day it was so nice he examined me physicaly 2 times then his son was with him he is Docktor too I was completely healthy I was so afraid I might have Consumtion I thought I was having such trouble breathing but the Docktor said that is because of my nerves so it will go away soon it is not so serious I have been getting medisine from Sister 3 times a day but now I am well so now I dont have to take it I think I am completely well now I am a little tired some times but I think I shall get better. The Docktor said I shall not be punished but I must go to hospital in stead then I can come back home to you it will be good again nice but then I have no children it will be so so hard I am not missing home but I am just missing and waiting for you hope you come to me soon Dear little Artur write and tell me if you were in Skövde on June 10th did we win anything in the lottery on May 15th now I am so glad because now my memory has come back it was completely gone when I was at Värnersborg then I could not remmember that I ever went to school now I remember every thing Docktor Golkhusl is so terribly kind I got candies from him 4 times them were so big and taste so good I also got a bunch of flowers from him that was blue flower violets them smell so good when it was Ingeborg day I got such lovely flowers from Sister and on my birithday Sister was off so I got flowers from Mrs Tor which she had picked in her own garden she is so kind

and now it will take 2 months for the papers to come from the Board of Meddisine I am still not shure of my punishment hoping for the best the Docktor said I will not have to go to Vänersborg that was so nice but perhaps I shall go to Ljung when the papers come back I hope I wont have to I had to do some drawing but it went badly but the sums went well then I had to read and then I got questions I had to go for 2 hours each time I was asked such funny questions some times but one evening I only got questions on that day I done such a bad thing it was so teribly hard then I was so upsett I couldnt sleep but at 11 the Nurse came with sleeping medicine but then I had such a sore head the next day that I nevver want any more I wish in stead it could of gone like Elsa said when she came in and saw what I done then the little children would of lived that was the dearest thing you had little Artur I think it is so sad for you but I nevver would of done it if I had not been ill read hynm 389 verse 2 and No. 599 1st verse I have read them many times I wish I didnt have to live any longer because now I shall nevver be at peace again I can nevver forget what I done am hoping the time will not be too long ask Farmor to foregive me for everything write soon dont forget me

A Lesson in Morality

Ingeborg was sitting in the far corner of the classroom, next to two large windows. They extended from floor to ceiling, occupying almost all of the short wall except for the ornate pillar in the middle, on which a round clock kept time as seconds, minutes and hours turned into days, weeks and years.

Pastor Virding, the chaplain, and Mrs Smedberg, the teacher, had developed the prison's education program and devised a broad and diverse curriculum. Mrs Smedberg taught astronomy, Swedish language and composition, history, mathematics, geography, literary and art history, civics, and hygiene. English lessons were split into a beginners' class and one for more advanced students. The governor's wife taught home economics, nutrition and cooking.

The chaplain provided religious and moral education, which consisted of instruction in Christian beliefs and ethics. He explained the meaning of Biblical revelations and Swedish hymns, and led singing lessons every Wednesday.

In this way, the chaplain did his best to combat the inner mendacity and wayward hearts of his charges, which he believed had led to their ruin. In his crusade against wickedness, he also held services three times a week and conducted 2,275 individual interviews with inmates.

In the classroom, the women each sat in their own cubicle, separated by tall wooden screens. The built-in desks were parallel to the long wall, facing the teacher's desk and the blackboard. The chaplain and the teacher could see the students, and the students could see them but not each other.

The cubicle next to Ingeborg was occupied by Emma, who, in her old age, had been convicted of embezzlement after being promoted to cashier. Emma had lost her mother and two sisters to the scarlet fever when it rampaged through their village in Dalarna.

Artur had come to congratulate Ingeborg on her twenty-second birthday. He stooped to avoid hitting his head on the door frame of the old cottage on the rocky hillside. The fir trees came right up to the house, sheltering it from the north wind. Artur knocked on the inner door of the hall before entering the dark kitchen.

"No need to knock," said Ingeborg's mother, getting up with difficulty to open the door.

"You'll be our son-in-law soon enough!"

Artur greeted Selma warmly. Ingeborg was sitting on the floor among a bundle of papers.

"Look what my sister found!" she said, holding up her old school report cards. "Didn't you run into her? She just went out to the barn to milk the cows."

"No, it's impossible to keep track of all your siblings," said Artur with a laugh.

"Yes, dear Lord!" sighed Selma, looking at her wrinkled hands. "This old woman bore and raised seven children, but soon all of them will have left home. How time flies!"

"I remember how terribly grand I thought your farm was when I used to walk by on my way to school," said Ingeborg, handing Artur a yellowed envelope.

"And now you're moving in there soon," said Selma. "Who would have ever thought it?"

Ingeborg and Artur had been an item since the barn dance organized by the local youth association the previous year. Mother Selma had been resolutely opposed to her going, but Ingeborg's father had talked her around, and eventually Ingeborg was allowed to go, with her sister as a chaperone.

"May I offer you a cup of coffee?" Selma continued.

"No, thanks, I can't stay long," replied Artur, sitting down beside Ingeborg on the floor and carefully unfolding one paper at a time.

Artur skimmed through the first report card, which was dated autumn 1908 in neat handwriting at top right.

"You weren't half bad at gymnastics and singing, I see."

Remembering the two fail grades she had received every term during her six years of schooling, Ingeborg suddenly became serious, and her cheeks flushed.

"I didn't mean to be unkind, Ingeborg," Artur hastened to add when he saw her reaction. "I was only teasing. Anyway, what use are screeching and running around? Diligence and good conduct are much more important, and there you got top marks. And in gardening too."

"Go on, won't you have a drop of coffee?" Selma persisted.

"Yes, why not, that's not such a bad idea after all," said Artur with a nod, smiling at his prospective mother-in-law as she lifted off a couple of hotplates with the poker and placed the coffee pot on the hearth.

They drank in silence. Ingeborg tried to forget her poor grades. Most of her seven classmates had fared poorly in history, geography and nature studies, but she had enjoyed school. She was never off sick for more than two or three of the eighty-plus schooldays in the year, and she was never absent without good reason.

"Did you have Miss Brandberg?" asked Artur after a while.

"Yes, she was such a lovely person," replied Ingeborg.

"You were really lucky," said Artur. "The other teacher was mean. She didn't quite beat us to pieces, but she certainly wasn't fair."

"I remember her, she lived with her mother. We used to call them 'the gentryfolk' because they were so haughty," said Ingeborg, bursting into a giggle. "But Miss Brandberg wasn't bothered in the least. She and her companion used to offer every visitor fruit juice and rusks, whether it was the pastor, the gentryfolk or the pauper."

"Did I ever tell you what that mean teacher did to my sister?" Artur asked, and Ingeborg shook her head. "My sister didn't care for needlework, and one day she pretended to have the sniffles so she could be excused from class. That turned out to be a mistake, because she got found out and was made to sew a handkerchief case as a punishment. There was a brand new sewing machine in the classroom, but only the best pupil was allowed to use it, so my sister ended up having to sew the whole thing by hand," said Artur, laughing.

In the cubicle the other side of Ingeborg, Ellen from Småland was gazing fondly at the chaplain. Little Ellen had been saved when she arrived at the prison, and the church service was her favourite part of the week. With her arms folded on the desk lid, as instructed, she was ready at any moment to raise her right forearm and answer the chaplain's questions on the Gospel and St Paul's epistles.

Ellen's mother had been caught unawares by a snowstorm on the way home from church when Ellen was barely six years old. Ellen's uncle had found the body the next day, after seeing a piece of cloth sticking out of a snowdrift when he was going out to fetch wood in the morning. He began digging and after a while discovered Ellen's mother frozen to death, clutching a hunk of bread.

As an adult, Ellen had taken to the drink with her husband. They always argued when playing cards in an advanced state of intoxication, and the last time they were seen together a shot had been fired. After that, the husband's spirits ration had been reduced from two litres to one litre, and Ellen was sent to Växjö. At least he had not received witness expenses like that wretch who impregnated three girls on Gotland and then abandoned them.

Among the inmates there were many nice girls who, unable to bear the shame of unmarried motherhood, had been driven to infanticide. Ellen was now teetotal and had not touched a drop of liquor for many a year. She looked forward to evening worship in the prison corridor, when the cell doors were cracked open and held ajar by a hook-and-eye arrangement known as the 'church hook'. This allowed her and the other inmates to hear the chaplain preaching from the centre of the mezzanine and to join in the hymns.

It was Wednesday afternoon, and the women had been expecting to watch *The Saga of Gösta Berling*, starring Greta Garbo. The teacher, who followed every step in the Hollywood career of the twenty-four-year-old actress, had managed to obtain a copy of the movie. She had wanted it to be a surprise, but could not contain herself and had told old Emma, and soon the whole prison knew of the plans. The chaplain had immediately called the whole thing off and was now going to talk about his walking tour of Rome instead.

The chaplain was a well-travelled man in his prime. At the age of thirty-seven, he had already studied the correctional systems of Denmark, Norway and Germany, got married, and been blessed with a son who was now eight years old.

"Even servile fear is better than unbridled freedom," declared the chaplain, beginning his slide show. "For I am appalled by the licentiousness of our times, in which men and women give free rein to their passions and carnal pleasures. I am appalled by how the ideal of purity is being abandoned and moral life is being corroded down to its innermost core."

The chaplain was projecting images of St Peter's Basilica and the Colosseum onto a large screen, using a magic lantern. The pastor back home had been intending to do likewise on his return from Italy, where he had celebrated his fiftieth birthday in the company of his wife and his brother-in-law Gustaf Dalén, the Nobel laureate. Ingeborg had been looking forward to the slide show at the poorhouse, but it had been cancelled because of an unexpected death in her family.

"Oh, is that the time?" the pastor in Vesene had said, putting his watch back in his breast pocket. "Then may I use your telephone?"

In the summer, the pastor usually cycled the nine kilometres between the parsonage and the five parishes in his charge, but in the winter the church's transport agreement with the local grocer came in handy.

Artur offered to make the call, and soon the only vehicle owner in the village arrived at the farm to drive the pastor to the church.

"It runs as smoothly as a sewing machine," said the grocer, tapping the steering wheel.

"I see," said the pastor distractedly.

The sexton's horse had been requisitioned for army service, so the pastor had to light the stove himself before the funeral guests arrived. Meanwhile, he was wondering what to say about Liss in his homily.

Växjö Jully 17th 1929 Wednesday

My Dear Artur,

I wanted to write you a few lines Thankyou for your letter believe me I was so happy yesterday when the Chaplin brought a letter from you I was so shure you had abandonned me when I nevver got a letter why didnt you write a few lines when you sent me the money but yesterday Sister went down and ask if any money had come for me that had arrived on June 18th I didnt know untill yesterday Thankyou for it and I got 5 kronor from Dagny and Karin and 5 kronor from Hilding 5 from Einar 2 kronor from Dagny apples and cookies from Elsa bananas candy and more goodies from Karin now I have 22 kronor to spend and then I ern 1.50 a week when I was 28 I got 10 kronor from Father and mother that was nice to get the pictures of the children but seeing them was so hard so I can not have them I send them back in this letter I didnt think seeing them woud be so hard as it was please send me in stead the picture you took that day Elsa went to America also the picture of the cottage that Beda took and the one Sjögård took when he was standing by the Church wall that is 3 pictures I want dont forget write soon and send them and then be so very very kind and come here when the hay making is finnished why did you not come at Midsummer like I wrote if you dont come then send my rings other wise bring them when you come they might get lost on the way you will come for shure and see how well I am you would nevver have thought it. The Docktor said he declared me fit now I will soon get my pappers back from Stockholm but the Docktor said I shall not be punished that was so nice now I go to class 1 and a half hours a day on tuesdays and thursdays we have no class at all on wendesday the Chaplin take the class for 2 hours then we have 1 hour bible studdy and then we read write sums then we learn about every thing then we get questions too I am in class 2 there are 4 clases 2 classes a day 12 at a time it is Mrs Smeberg who teach the classes she is higher than a school teacher it is so nice believe me we can only sit one at each desk we can not see each other we have 1 each now I weigh 60 kilos when I came here I weigh 53 kilos believe me I am plump and fat Imagin if I could come to you with this letter I will not write more this time because I want you to come here as soon as you can I just miss you come here for shure write soon if you are coming or not I wrote to mother yesterday she is 66 on sunday Much love to all of you kind wishes from Ingeborg come for sure Artur

there are 11 of us all together 8 are up 3 are still in bed I can not forget what I done I thinkt about you every night and Morning. do not forget me dear Artur.

hope you come to me soon I am expecting you My dear Artur Just think how nice it will be to see you and talk to you. write soon dont forget I beg you Ingeborg

A Visit

"How are things?"

Artur pulled out the wooden chair and sat down opposite his wife at a small rectangular table in the centre of the large visiting hall. On his left arm was a black mourning band. A crumpled white shirt could be glimpsed under his overcoat, and he was wearing a white bow tie around the turned-up collar.

"I'm doing pretty well, thank you," said Ingeborg, fidgeting with the three empty wooden frames in front of her. "Won't you take off your overcoat?"

"I'm not going to be long," replied Artur, getting up anyway and draping his coat over the back of the chair.

"How was your journey?"

"The train was held up between Herrljunga and Borås, so I thought I was going to miss my connection at Alvesta, but the Växjö train waited for us."

"It's a shame you were delayed. I hope we can get a better spot next time," said Ingeborg, looking at the girl sitting at one of the corner tables.

Ingeborg didn't know her, but knew she was from Malmö. She was usually confined to bed, but was now sitting hunched forward, whispering to a well-dressed older couple. Hearing the Skåne burr when they spoke, Ingeborg surmised that the visitors were the girl's parents.

"I was so sure you had abandoned me," Ingeborg continued.

Artur was clean-shaven but had bags under his eyes. Since Ingeborg last saw him, he had changed his hairstyle. His thick dark hair was now parted evenly in the centre, instead of being parted on the left. She wondered whether he still carried a comb in the back pocket of his good trousers.

"If the postage hadn't been so awfully expensive, I would have sent them with my last letter," said Ingeborg, pushing the frames across the table. "You can have them for the photos of the children, as your brother intended. How is Holger?"

"He's given up driving."

Ingeborg tried to catch Artur's weary eye, but he continued staring down at the table. He smelled of aftershave and shoe polish.

"And Elsa? Has she gone back to America yet?"

"Mother wants her to stay at home now," said Artur, falling silent.

He gently touched the smallest frame. Then he bent down and picked up his rucksack off the floor, opened it, and produced a jar of raw lingonberry jam.

"Star calved yesterday."

"No!" exclaimed Ingeborg, reaching out to her husband.

"Mother made a beestings pancake for supper," said Artur, ignoring Ingeborg's hand. "She was afraid it would turn sour in transit, otherwise she would have sent you a piece to have with the jam."

"That would have been so delicious!"

"Aren't you dressed yet?" Farmor had asked Tor when she entered the kitchen, in the week when Liss passed away. "Have you had anything to eat?"

"No," Tor had answered.

"Where is your mother?"

Tor had presumably pointed to the parlour, because shortly afterwards Farmor opened the door. It smelled stuffy, like the granary in the summer when the grain was running low and there was mainly old dust left in the bins. Farmor bent over, picked up the scissors and the rag strips, and put them on the corner table next to a withered begonia. She touched the plant's dry soil with her finger and went back into the kitchen to fetch a watering can. After tending to the plant, she walked over to Ingeborg, who was sitting at the loom with her fingers on the warp. Farmor looked at the half-finished rug and carefully picked up the shuttle from her daughter-in-law's lap.

"That one will fetch a good bit extra. Is that rosepath?" inquired Farmor, but Ingeborg made no reply.

"Shall I help you into the bedroom?" asked Farmor. "You'll feel better if you put some proper clothes on."

Mrs Appelgren was guarding the entrance to the visiting hall. There was a knock, and she opened the door to Sister Gunhild, who was bringing a tray of coffee.

"I see we have company from afar. How nice!" said Sister Gunhild, stopping at Artur and Ingeborg's table. "Are you staying overnight in Växjö, Mr Andersson?"

"No, I need to get home to the animals."

"Star has just calved," added Ingeborg.

"Is that so?" said Sister Gunhild, serving the coffee. "Hope you enjoy it."

"Thank you," said Artur before the nurse moved on to the next table. "I'm sure we shall."

Ingeborg and Artur drank in silence. Ingeborg wanted to tell him about Dr Goldkuhl and all the new things she had learned. She wanted to tell him about old Emma and little Ellen. About the walks outside and the teacher. But she didn't know where to begin, or how to explain.

"Ingeborg."

"Yes, Artur dear."

Ingeborg thought it was almost like being back home at the kitchen table. With the nurserymaid, Liss and Farmor. The children playing noisily. The thud of the loom. The ticking of the American clock. The nurserymaid frying pork with Lucia on her arm.

"I think about you and the children a lot," said Artur, taking a deep breath. "It's not good to brood as much as I do. I don't want to end up like your father."

Artur looked at Ingeborg's outstretched hand, but could not bring himself to reach out and hold it.

"The pastor says you didn't know what you were doing and I must forgive you and God for what happened in order to keep going," Artur continued, running a hand across his face. "I am really trying, Ingeborg, but the house is so empty and silent without the children."

"Yes, they were full of life, those little children," said Ingeborg. "My goodness, our nurserymaid had her work cut out. She was too willing."

"If my uncle moves in with us, I'm moving out to the barn with the cat," Liss had said, embracing the nurserymaid from behind. "Unless I can move in with you, of course."

"I'm not sure that would be a wise move," said Artur.

"Don't you ever shut up? Now you're embarrassing me in front of Mr Andersson again. Here, take the wee one from me, will you? The fat is splashing so much I'm worried she'll get burnt."

"If only you were fond of me, then I could help you with the milking," said Liss, taking Lucia in his arms.

"I'd sooner die."

"As long as I close the latch from inside, no-one will notice the man of the house doing women's work."

"Man of the house?" said the nurserymaid, rolling her eyes. "Go and change your trousers! I can smell the manure on you a mile away."

"What's that you're saying about your uncle?" asked Artur.

"His fiancée has called off the engagement. If he was stubborn before, he's seven times worse now. Dad says that Grandma and Grandpa can't allow him to live at home any longer."

"Then they should move him out to the barn, not you," said Artur, laughing.

"Who is it that's moving?" inquired Farmor as she entered the kitchen.

Before Artur or Liss had a chance to reply, Farmor went over to the stove and stole a piece of pork from the frying pan.

"I've brought some chair covers for the parlour," she went on, showing them the package under her arm, "but I couldn't resist having a taste while I'm here. Goodness me, that smells good!"

"Of course you can try the pork," replied the nurserymaid, as Farmor told them the pastor had posted an announcement about Sunday school on the district notice board on the church wall.

"You'll soon be old enough to start going," she told Tor, patting her grandson on the head.

"I brought your rings as you asked me to in your letter," said Artur, taking a folded handkerchief out of his jacket pocket.

Ingeborg undid the little bundle and put one of the gold rings on her right forefinger, spinning it round and round and round. She left the other ring in the handkerchief.

"They need cleaning," said Ingeborg. "It's been ages since I did it. Perhaps Sister Gunhild can help me."

"Ingeborg, I —"

Artur got no further. Visiting time was over. He tied the drawstrings on his rucksack and closed the flap. Ingeborg noticed a pale band that had not caught the sun on his left ring finger. Artur put his coat on and shook his wife's hand awkwardly.

"Don't forget me," she whispered.

As Artur left the visiting hall, Ingeborg went over to the big window and watched him walking across the courtyard on his way to the station. The sun, already low in the sky, had yet to dry out the ground after the first frost of autumn. The shadows cast by the well-groomed red and yellow tree formed a sombre silhouette behind him as the first fall leaves drifted gently to earth. Ingeborg waved, but Artur did not look back.

"Now my hardest road awaits me," she thought.

Växjö September 1st 1929

My dear little Artur

Dear Artur I just wanted to write a few lines to say thankyou for coming here believe me it was nice that you came but it was so sad when you left. Imagin if I could of come home with you but I hope that day will come some time all tho it will probably be awhile but then it will be nice to be with you all of the time. And be able to help you. Imagin if that day come soon. It is so nice that

I am so well now and I sleep so well at night from 9 o clock to 6 o clock everyday. I have now finnished Astrid cardigin it turn out so lovely believe me. Dagny will be happy when she gets it I shall send it this week it only cost 60 öre for the postage I shall croshay a cardigin and a shaul for me, then the time will go quick I think oh if only it was Christmas soon so you would come here I am already expecting you. when you went away it was so sad after. come at Christmas for sure I am expecting you. did the journey home go well did you then visit Ebba and Nils.

now the Docktor has been on his holidays for a month then we had another Docktor from Växjö hospital he has been here twice then on Sunday there was Holy Comunnion in the church it was so formal we got to sit down in the church there were 35 of us we sat one in each pew we had to sit the whole time. Here it is so nice to go to classes here now I am expecting a letter from mother it is 3 weeks since I wrote to her Were you at Intabo on Thursday tell me when you write to me. Now there is a court hearing in Ljung on September 3rd I do not have to go there that was so nice write if you were there. Did you see me waving out the windo when you walked down the street now we are allowed to have lights on untill 9 o clock that is so nice when we are at church in the evenings then there are so many lamps burning it is so lovely The day after you left there were 8 Gentlemen here from Stockholm inspeckting the Infirmary.

Much love to all of you at Haggården give Ester and the little children at Klockaregården my love. Write soon that would be so terribly kind I am expecting a letter

kind wishes from Ingeborg

dont forget to write soon I am expecting a letter.

Restad Manor

"I need to speak to Ingeborg, please," said Dr Goldkuhl, peeking into the day room.

Five inmates looked up from their aprons in surprise, momentarily losing concentration on their woven ribbons to stare at the prison doctor, who was standing in the doorway waving a large brown envelope.

"Let's go to your room, Ingeborg, where we can talk in peace," the doctor continued.

When they reached Ingeborg's cell, he took out the letter and read it aloud:

Whereas Ingeborg Maria Andersson, by her own admission, supported by the facts of the case, has been lawfully convicted of having, on March 22, 1929, with malice aforethought, killed her three children, Tor, Efraim and Lucia, by drowning them in a copper washtub filled with water, the District Court finds that Mrs Andersson has accepted responsibility in accordance with chapter 14, section 1, of the Penal Code, but inasmuch as Mrs Andersson, according to the opinion issued by the National Board of Medicine on August 16, 1929, was not of sound mind at the time of committing these acts, owing to mental illness, the District Court lawfully declares that, the acts being unpunishable under chapter 5, section 5, of the Penal Code, Mrs Andersson cannot be held criminally responsible in this case; in consequence whereof she shall no longer be held in custody but is to be handed over to the relevant Crown authority to receive such care as may be necessary to prevent her from becoming a danger to public safety.

"That's good news, isn't it? Now we can finally request a hospital place for you," exclaimed Dr Goldkuhl, unable to contain his excitement at Tuesday's verdict from Gäsene courthouse.

The doctor was still standing in front of the closed door, looking searchingly at Ingeborg, who was sitting quietly on the edge of the bed with her hands in her lap. She blushed, feeling embarrassed for the doctor.

"It will be like living on a farm," said Dr Goldkuhl enthusiastically. "Even better, in fact. A country estate! Before Restad Manor became a hospital, it was the summer residence of the county governor. But, needless to say, it's a big hospital," the doctor went on, somewhat more pensively. "A thousand patients, one of the biggest in the country."

A thousand patients, thought Ingeborg. More than twice as many people as in the entire parish of Vesene.

"What, have you come sniffing around for corpses?" Ivar had said to the undertaker from Vesene when Ingeborg came back into the church after throwing up in the churchyard.

The undertaker had pushed his way to the front, even though the verger had gently pointed out that the nave was full but there was plenty of space in the gallery.

"Well, well, Ivar, what are you doing back home? Have the fine gentlemen of the district council still not managed to buy you a one-way ticket to the madhouse in Vänersborg?" replied the undertaker, thumping Ivar on the back so hard that Efraim, who was sitting beside him on Artur's lap, had woken up and started crying. "Perhaps I need to get involved in politics again to bring a little law and order to this parish."

Artur rocked the child and pretended not to have heard.

"Where the hell has that priest got to?" the undertaker went on.

"Here he is," said the plump pastor calmly, emerging from the sacristy.

"Don't swear in church!" yelled Ivar.

He was flushed with aggravation. The pastor looked up from his Bible, and the music fell silent. The undertaker waved his left hand irritatedly in Ivar's direction, as if the old man was a horsefly in a hayloft.

"Don't swear in church, I said!"

Ingeborg could still remember the passing whiff of breakfast eggs, and how she held up her hand to shield herself from any more regurgitated food that might come flying past.

"Bloody village idiot!" the undertaker had cried, shoving Ivar in the chest so hard that he lost his balance and collapsed in the pew.

"That was uncalled for," Artur had mumbled, taking Ivar by the arm to help him up.

"I don't mean nobody no harm. It just pains me so sore when he swears in church."

"Come on, I'll take you home," said the verger, but Ivar would not let go of Artur's arm.

"Now they will send me away to Restad again," he had snivelled. "I don't want to go back there. Please, don't let them send me back to Vänersborg."

"Restad Hospital consists of thirty brick buildings and is really more like a large village," said Dr Goldkuhl, seeing the concern on Ingeborg's face. "You will soon feel at home, Ingeborg, as soon as you've got used to the new routine. I'm certain of that."

Dr Goldkuhl sat down beside her on the edge of the bed and patted her hand. He talked about the modern, humane care regime that the hospital had offered since it opened twenty-five years ago. He took out some photographs showing the beautiful location on the banks of the Göta River. He pointed out the kitchen garden that kept the patients supplied with apples, currants, rhubarb and strawberries in the summer. He told her about the hospital's chickens and pigs, the tailoring shop and the brewery. There was even a bakery, and he had heard that the old baking ovens had been replaced with electric tunnel ovens last year, and that the bakery was now supplying bread to another hospital as well.

"But best of all, Ingeborg, is that you will be living so much nearer to Artur," said Dr Goldkuhl. "Vänersborg is little more than an hour's journey from Vesene, so I'm sure you will find that he visits you much more often than he does here."

Växjö, Sept. 17th 1929

My dear little Artur

Dear little Artur I just wanted to write you a few lines. I am now expecting a letter from you did you not get the letter I sent you a fourtnight ago. Hope you are well I am so well. I would be really glad if you could send me 10 kronor because I have now bought yarn for my cardigin for 10 kronor it cost for 800 grams 1.25 a ball it is so fun to croshay I have to croshay for another week before it is finnished it is grey that is such a lovely colour, I think, then I was thinking I would buy yarn to knit socks for you. When I finnished them you can come here and get them so I dont have to send them in the post. I am looking fourward to you coming as it is so nice when you come here. Now you probabbly have lots to do with the harvest, have you harvested the oats yet, here the weather is so fine and warm during the day hope it is the same for you too, here they harvested the grain allready. Imagin if I could of come to you with this letter that would of been nice. hope that day come soon that will be nice. Now Pastor Verding has come come back here. We had him in class the first time on Wednesday. Now we do not have Pastor Samuelsson anymore. Now I go to cooking class 2 days a week Monday and Tuesday 10 til 11 o clock each day it is Governors Wife who teach cooking class we have to write down recipees in a book we get to keep. I wrote to Karin that I would like Karin and Lylli to come here in the fall. I got a letter from Karin the other week but she said nothing about it It would be so nice if they would come and see me. Please remind Karin about it. Have you been home to see Mother and Father since you saw me let them know I am feeling so well Give my regard to Miss Stenborg and thank her for every thing I have not written to her I think I write so ugly, so I dont want to write to her Let her know I am so well regard to Miss Branberg. she feels so sorry for you. I got a letter from Dagny she had been to Mollaskoga picking rasberries Karin and Lylly then she met Mrs Bertilsson she asked her to give me her regards give her mine If

Ebba in Borås had known Dagny and Karin were coming here she would of come with them she said
Much love to all of you at Haggårn
kind wishes from Ingeborg Andersson

did you buy cloth for Sigge at Klockaregården did Ingrid get it from you

write soon and dont forget to send money. I am expecting it now. dear little Artur I miss you so much my dear Artur did you not get my letter or have you no time to write I am expecting a letter Regards Ingeborg

dont forget me your dear Ingeborg

Imagin if you could come to me this Sunday

Christmas

The twin towers of Växjö cathedral loomed brick red against the grey vault of the sky. Large snowflakes were falling around them, like glitter in a snow globe. The hill leading up to the cathedral was littered with smoking torches left behind by the congregation after the early morning service. Ingeborg was sitting up in bed, thumbing at an old letter from Dr Oliver Ottosson, chief physician at Restad Hospital, as the church bells rang in Christmas.

I respectfully beg to inform you that Ingeborg Maria Andersson, who has been declared not criminally responsible, and in respect of whom we have received an application for hospital care, cannot expect to be admitted to this institution in the immediate future, owing to lack of capacity.

The church bells of Gothenburg had also been ringing for the early morning service on May 8, 1923, when Ingeborg threw open the glazed doors to the french balcony at the Hotel Bungalow. The sun was blazing and the stench from the sewers engulfed her. She had not slept a wink all night, being unused to all the new sounds. She was fascinated by the big city and leaned over the Art Nouveau railings to watch the crowds. The double room with ensuite bathroom, costing 18 kronor a night, overlooked Parkgatan, the street along which the citizens were making their way to Central Station to welcome King Gustav V and Queen Victoria. Mounted police constables in spiked helmets and double-breasted overcoats, carrying swords, were maintaining law and order. Blue-and-yellow flags were flying from hundreds of flagpoles.

"Be careful!" Artur had called, grabbing her nightgown. "Don't you see how high up we are? If you fall off, you'll die instantly."

"Don't be so worried about me, Artur dear," said Ingeborg. "Come on, let's go and greet the King too. That would be such fun!"

Artur put the admission tickets to the city's tercentennial celebration in his wallet and donned his new fedora. Ingeborg was wearing a wide-brimmed straw hat decorated with flowers. After glancing in the mirror, they ventured downstairs to the hotel's lavish breakfast buffet.

"This is grander than the City Hotel in Borås," whispered Ingeborg as the bellboy pushed the revolving door and they wandered out into the throng, arm in arm.

The sidewalk was crowded. All of Gothenburg, almost a quarter of a million people, seemed to be heading for the station to welcome the royal patrons of the Jubilee Exhibition. A clattering streetcar bound for the seaside kept ringing its bell to make the crowds move out of its way. A barge carrying coal and sand was traversing the canal. Smoke was billowing from the chimneys, and Artur pulled out his chequered snuff handkerchief and handed it to Ingeborg to shield her face with. Cranes rattled in the nearby harbour. On the station platform, white handkerchiefs fluttered in the wind as the royal entourage alighted from the Stockholm train. In the distance, the cannons on Kvarnberget fired a traditional Swedish royal salute.

The King and Queen rode in a cab to Brunnsparken, where they laid a wreath at the statue of the city's founder. A grand cortege then proceeded up Kungsportsavenyn, past Kopparmärra, to the main entrance to the Jubilee Exhibition beside the fountain on Götaplatsen. Gustav V declared the exhibition open, and four trumpeters blared out a fanfare. Ingeborg and Artur walked past the pond of white waterlilies and up the steep slope to the handicrafts pavilion.

"Imagine being able to sew like that," remarked Ingeborg as they passed a cross-stitched wall hanging.

After a couple of hours, Artur was starting to grow impatient, but Ingeborg could not tear herself away from the films featuring the latest weaving techniques.

"My goodness, there is so much to see, it is unbelievable!" she exclaimed, and Artur resigned himself to looking at the cars the next day.

The voice of Jussi Björling rang out from the gramophone in the corridor, awakening Ingeborg from her daydreams. The National Board of Corrections had sent a worldly gift to the inmates of the infirmary that Christmas. In the echo chamber of the prison, the tenor vied for attention with the clatter of cups from the kitchen. The smell of coffee wound its way up the spiral staircase and the light shaft to the third floor and under the door of Ingeborg's cell.

"I am not worthy of being in the house of God," whispered Ingeborg, pursing her lips to hold back the tears as Dr Goldkuhl knocked on her door.

"Why do you say that?"

"He didn't come," said Ingeborg. "Artur didn't come."

"Christmas is not over yet. I'm sure Artur will come and visit you tomorrow or the day after, just you wait and see. There, wipe away those tears. I'll come with you to the Christmas service."

Dr Goldkuhl took Ingeborg's arm and led her to the prison chapel. They sat with the other unrestricted inmates in the gallery, just as the organist struck up the opening notes of *Hosanna, Son of David*. The square sanctuary below them looked empty and desolate, except for the chaplain, who was pacing back and forth in front of the olive green and gold wooden cross, ringing a small brass bell on a worn wooden handle. The prisoners hid in their wooden cubicles, invisible to themselves and each other even on Christmas Eve.

As the tones of the visiting city choir faded away, the chaplain read from chapter two of the Gospel according to St Luke: "For unto you is born this day in the city of David a Saviour, which is Christ the Lord. And this shall be a sign unto you; Ye shall find the babe wrapped in swaddling clothes, lying in a manger."

The starched white clerical collar beneath his pointed chin bobbed up and down as he spoke. Usually the chaplain talked about Order, Cleanliness and Tidiness, about the value of a regular and proper way of living, fixed routines and good literature, by which he meant religious texts primarily, and secondly more general educational texts. He usually spoke about the joy and blessing of work, but today was a day of rest and his sermon was about Peace. Peace on Earth and Jesus our Saviour, *Iesus Hominum Salvator, IHS*, as was written on the purple altar frontal.

Ingeborg looked out of the window. It was already dark outside, but it was not as draughty as usual. It felt as if the whole building was wrapped in a thick, black felt blanket. A massive Christmas tree, decorated with garlands and crowned with two Swedish flags, spread a dim light and the scent of spruce needles through the prison corridor on the two upper levels.

The cows chewing the cud behind the barbed wire fence had approached the farmhouse as Artur and Ingeborg came running down the churchyard hill. Hand in hand, they took a shortcut across the neighbour's field for the final stretch. The fishpond had overflowed after recent downpours, and the grass was springy under their feet as they scampered along. Ingeborg missed a tussock, and the sodden ground gave way as she landed in the adjacent puddle. The water seeped slowly into the thin cloth shoes that her father had bought from a hawker the week before. She looked on in alarm as a light brown stain spread over the tongue and heel.

"Come on!" called Artur, who was already there.

Ingeborg hurried the last few steps, and Artur opened the black iron gate to his splendid farm. With twelve dairy cows, four heifers, a bull, three pigs, sixty chickens and two horses, and 135 acres of land, it was the biggest farm in the village. The tame cattle, which were staring at them between a couple of birch trees that had just come into leaf, recoiled at the noise of metal hitting metal when Artur let go of the gate latch too soon. The freshly raked gravel path crunched beneath their feet as they approached the white glazed veranda.

"Close your eyes," said Artur, holding his hands over Ingeborg's face.

Intertwined, they stumbled across the threshold of the newly renovated farmhouse.

"Now you can open them," whispered Artur, removing his hands.

Ingeborg found herself, open-mouthed, in a large, bright kitchen. The door to the bedroom was wide open, and she could see through to the parlour. There was a smell of soap and freshly picked lilies of the valley. Ingeborg twirled around, held her hand to her mouth and exclaimed:

"It's absolutely beautiful, Artur! It almost seems a shame to live here, it's so beautiful."

Then she remembered her wet shoes and hurried out the back door to leave them on the stoop, holding on to the ornately carved railing crafted last century by a carpenter giving free rein to his creativity.

"Aren't you going to take off your boots too, Artur dear?" she inquired on her return. "It would be a pity if we messed up the freshly scrubbed floor."

Artur followed her example, while she took a handkerchief out of her pinafore and bent down to wipe away their footprints.

Ingeborg dried her eyes and tried to concentrate on the Christmas carol.

In one of the wooden cubicles below, old Emma sneezed and blew her nose loudly.

"Bless you!" whispered little Ellen, hushing her.

A tallow candle illuminated Ingeborg's flushed face. On her lap, under her hymn book, she was hiding her Christmas present from Governor Fehrnström: a beautifully bound Christmas magazine with illustrations by Jenny Nyström. She touched the cellophane wrapper lightly, reverently, and it crackled, causing her to withdraw her hand in alarm. She gazed at the dark red bow and thought about the Christmas star waiting in her cell.

"The grace of Our Lord Jesus Christ be with you all." The chaplain finished his sermon, and the organist played the introduction to the final carol.

Silent night! Holy night!
All is calm, all is bright

> Round yon virgin mother and child;
> Holy infant, so tender and mild,
> Sleep in heavenly peace,
> Sleep in heavenly peace.

"Mother whitewashed the stove tiles and I put up the wood panelling," Artur had explained on his return, pressing a black knob in the middle of the wall.

"Goodness, my dear Artur, surely you haven't put in electric power?"

"Yes I have, the first house in the village! I went to the power station and signed up for nine electric lights and bought three shares in the company for a hundred riksdaler. Then Holger helped me put up the poles for the power line."

"I'd never have imagined you and your brother were so clever. I can hardly believe it!" Ingeborg exclaimed, clapping her hands.

"No, it seemed like a distant prospect, but I'm not one to give up easily. Remember how our neighbour blustered and swore he was going to stop me?"

"Yes, how could I forget?"

"Artur is not going to run one single power line past this farm! I'll stake my head on it!" mimicked Artur, putting on a whiny voice. "But then I told him that his head probably wasn't worth a great deal. Remember that, Ingeborg? He had already wagered it that time he led the protests against the soldier's croft and lost at every stage, all the way up to the Supreme Court."

"You're so clever, Artur! But you've made up with him now, haven't you?" she asked apprehensively.

"Sort of. He's not easy to get along with, believe me."

"Perhaps you could just show him how well it works?"

"No, that's not a good idea. He has taken it into his head that electricity is the work of the devil. But he might come if we threw an electric light party."

"Amen," said the chaplain, blowing out the candle.

Ingeborg stood up, and the superintendent accompanied her back to her cell. Suddenly a woman started yelling and banging on her cell door with both hands.

"Hello! In here!"

"What is it, my dear?" inquired the superintendent.

"The guard locked my door after the Christmas service, even though he knows I only have to have the latch on."

"Oh, is that all?"

"All? I'll have you know, it felt like the whole cell was closing in. Is the coffee coming any time soon?"

"Coffee," said Ingeborg.

The superintendent looked up in surprise and started laughing.

"That certainly perked you up, didn't it, Mrs Andersson? You and Emma will get a cup soon, I promise."

Växjö, February 3rd

My dear little Artur

First of all thankyou for the money you send me, I would of written before, but I was waiting for a letter from you. I keep wondering why I don't hear nothing from you, you did forgive me one time for what I done. You must think something of me that it all can be well again. The Docktor has said I am so well now, that I can come home soon, I am so glad believe me. it is going quicker than I thought myself. I got permision from the Doctor to go out for awhile and Sister Gunhild took me home for coffee it was so nice, to go out to the town, you would nevver believe it. It would be so nice if you would accept me, in good faith, dear little Artur and all was well betwen us again. I should be pleased if you would write a reply to this letter so I could hear from you.

Much fond love from your Ingeborg.

Farewell

"My dear Ingeborg, what is wrong?" inquired Dr Goldkuhl as he entered Ingeborg's room.

"To think that I killed my children, even though I loved them dearly! I don't know what to do with myself, wretched woman that I am! I shall never be saved."

Ingeborg was sitting on the edge of the bed, weeping, her head bowed and her hands folded. Dr Goldkuhl sat down beside her. He took her hand in his and held it to his cheek. Ingeborg stole a glance at him and fidgeted with her apron in embarrassment, pinching a fold in the fabric and running her fingers back and forth along it.

"I don't know how I could have done it," she went on. "I felt nothing at the time. Such a strong temptation just came to me on a whim. I was not thinking about anything. I was compelled, but I don't know where the compulsion came from."

"I understand, Ingeborg. I understand."

"It is so hard. I have such strange thoughts. Thoughts that stand still. Lost children whom I loved so dearly!"

"I'm so sorry I have neglected you recently, Ingeborg," said Dr Goldkuhl. "Please understand that this had nothing to do with you. I haven't been too well, you see."

Ingeborg looked up. If she hadn't known better, she would have believed that the man was crying, that they were sitting together on the edge of the bed in her cell and weeping. Dr Goldkuhl cleared his throat.

"But today I bring good news," he continued, handing Ingeborg an envelope.

Ingeborg opened the letter from Dr Ottosson, chief physician, and read that she had finally been allocated a place at Restad Hospital.

A month later, Dr Goldkuhl accompanied Ingeborg and the custody officer to the station. When it was time to say goodbye, the doctor took his patient's hand and shook it slowly for a long time. Ingeborg recalled another farewell in another time.

"I need to speak to you, ma'am," the nurserymaid had said, knocking on the parlour door.

When no reply came, she had cautiously cracked open the door and peeked in. Ingeborg was sitting at the bench of the loom, hunched over like an old woman.

"I can't stay on any longer," the nurserymaid whispered, burying her face in her apron. "I'm awfully fond of the children, but I just can't stand it anymore."

Lucia, who had crawled across the floor to her guardian angel, grabbed hold of the girl's skirt and reached up with one hand. The nurserymaid picked her up in her arms and swallowed.

"I'm swallowing to clear the lump in my throat. Swallowing my rage and anger at Liss leaving me. Several months have now passed, but I can't keep on swallowing any longer. I can't bear any more sorrow. Liss is everywhere here. I see him by the stove, in the woodshed, in the children. It's like he is there in the walls, ma'am. I need to get away from him, from this family, from this village. I need to start over. Somewhere else."

"Oh, for the chance to start over," replied Ingeborg. "I miss him too. Liss was like a brother to me."

Ingeborg got up and walked toward the kitchen door. The nurserymaid followed and stood on the steps outside in her stocking feet, with Lucia on her arm and Efraim clinging to one leg. Tor stayed in the hall, hesitating.

"I've been offered a job in Vänersborg. They want me to start next week," the nurserymaid went on.

"Then I wish you all the best," said Ingeborg, heading across the grass to the outhouse.

"I promise I'll come back and visit!" the nurserymaid called after her, but Ingeborg didn't hear as she stood right beneath the drip from the eaves, tugging at the wooden door, which had swollen in the heavy autumn rains and was now hard to open.

The gutter was overflowing, and Ingeborg nearly fell over as the door finally yielded and swung open. She sat down beside one of the four holes and closed the latch from inside.

When Dr Goldkuhl eventually let go of Ingeborg's hand, she turned around and stepped out onto the platform toward the train. Taking hold of the handrail, she was about to mount the steps when she stopped and turned her head to look at him. He had taken his hat off and was holding it in front of him with both hands.

"Are you feeling better now, Dr Goldkuhl?" she asked.

"Yes, thank you, Ingeborg, I am feeling a little better now. But some wounds never heal. I'm sure you know what I mean. My wife passed away on the third of November. She was only fifty-four. Sometimes life doesn't turn out how you had imagined."

Throughout her imprisonment, Ingeborg was kind, appreciative and respectful, wrote Dr Goldkuhl on Ingeborg's chart when he returned to the prison.

A Burlap Bath Cover

The custody officer was holding Ingeborg by the arm. Side by side, they walked up the avenue bordering the extensive lawn that separated the women's pavilion on the north side from the men's annex to the south. With their straight gravel paths, circles and rhododendron bushes, the landscaped grounds resembled a circular, open labyrinth or an overgrown baroque garden. The central axis extended from the main hospital building in front of them, past the stores and administration building behind them, and all the way down to the bathing jetty by the river.

The matron was standing on the stone steps at the main entrance, her folded hands resting against her freshly ironed white apron. She wore a navy blue knitted cardigan around her shoulders.

"Welcome," she said, extending her hand.

Ingeborg made no reply. She was looking down at her shoe and poking at a couple of pebbles in the gravel path. Two orderlies positioned themselves on either side of her and took hold of her waist and an arm each, before leading her up the steps between them. The custody officer hastened back to the waiting car that would take her back to the prison in the town centre. The matron nodded goodbye and placed the key in the lock of the heavy wooden door.

"Please take a seat," said the matron, pointing to an empty chair, when they reached the admission room on the second floor.

The matron opened her book of charts and flipped through a dozen pages until she came to patient number 2826: Ingeborg Maria Andersson, admitted April 1, 1930. She had already entered Ingeborg's personal details and information from her trial, physical examination and psychiatric evaluation on a new page.

"I see you are from Vesene, Mrs Andersson," she said, looking over her glasses. "Perhaps you know Ivar, who is one of our residents here?"

Ivar had been sitting on his kitchen steps with a bare chest, sharing a quarter-bottle of hard liquor with the village tailor when the procession of mourners walked past the almshouse on their way up the avenue to the church.

"Poor dear, she'll never get the washing dry in this cold," Mother Selma had sighed when she saw Ivar's daughter hanging out a load of sheets and underwear on the bushes.

"Doing laundry on a Sunday! What the hell are they playing at?" exclaimed the undertaker.

"Can't you see that the girl is trying to clean up after her father?" replied Farmor. "I don't think you could put up with that pigsty for long either."

Artur raised his hat to Ivar's daughter and then approached the two drunks.

"Want a swig?"

"No, thank you, maybe another time."

"Liss was a fine lad," said Ivar, putting the bottle down before wiping his right hand on his filthy trousers and extending it in greeting.

"We need to repave the bridge over the river. The village residents have to pave six feet each, and I could use the help of a skilled handyman," said Artur.

"Then you're talking to the right man," said Ivar, brightening up.

"If you can remove the rotten timbers and install three new joists before laying the planks, I'll feed you and pay you a decent wage."

"You can trust me. If you provide the oak logs and the nails, I'll also saw you a couple of aspens for the handrail into the bargain."

Artur raised his hat and was about to leave when Ivar began scratching and beating his chest.

"Oh, I just had a visitor," said Ivar, taking off his coat and pulling out a frightened mouse.

When the matron received no reply, she took out a craniometer, measured the length and width of Ingeborg's skull, and calculated the skull index. She looked at the resulting number with satisfaction and entered it on the chart, adding the comment: *No abnormalities in head shape or size.*

"Now all you need is a cleansing bath," she said, ringing a small brass bell.

A strongly built, late-middle-aged woman wearing a black oilskin coat with rolled-up sleeves and knee-high rubber boots appeared in a doorway on the far left of the room.

Ingeborg shuddered, noticing for the first time that there was another door behind the desk.

"Take off your clothes," ordered the woman.

Ingeborg was staring down at the striped rag rug in shades of light blue on the floor.

"You can leave your clothes and belongings on the chair here, and I'll register them and put them away for safekeeping," said the matron.

When Ingeborg failed to respond, the strongly built woman grabbed hold of her feet and pulled off her galoshes.

"Get up!"

Ingeborg held the arms of the chair in a vicelike grip, hearing nothing, seeing nothing. The orderlies grabbed her arms, lifted her out of the chair, and held her still while the large woman removed her boa and coat.

"You were lucky to be admitted, Ingeborg. Our waiting time is currently seven months for non-urgent cases," said the matron, flicking through the pages of the chart.

The woman unbuttoned Ingeborg's cardigan and skirt and handed them to the matron. In return she received a bundle of clothes, which she placed on the table beside the visitor's chair.

"Because we are over capacity, the laundry can't keep up," explained the matron without looking up from her papers. "We are short of clothes for patients, so you will have to wear an old staff uniform for the time being, Mrs Andersson."

The woman continued to undress Ingeborg, one garment after another, until only a pale, naked female body remained, already stooped at the age of twenty-eight. Ingeborg had been needing to go to the bathroom all day, but could not bring herself to ask, and could hold on no longer. There was something warm trickling down her thigh. She was back in Vesene, at home with her father, standing in the middle of the bedroom. She was ten years old and had just had an accident. She was unable to move. Her father was down on the floor, mopping up after her. Ten years old. She was a big girl. Almost a grown-up.

"These things happen," her father had said. "Let's just forget about it and not tell your mother."

"The woman led the naked figure past the matron into the adjoining room, where she inspected Ingeborg's body.

"No wounds, rashes or lice," she confirmed, pushing Ingeborg into the bathtub in front of them.

The water was warm, and for a while Ingeborg forgot about the woman and the coarse brush scrubbing her skin till it was red. She forgot about the blue and white chequered cotton dress. She forgot about the orderly putting the white kerchief on her after they had washed her hair. She forgot that only unmarried women were allowed to wear their hair down.

"The photographer is waiting," said the matron, tying Ingeborg's white apron with a bow at the back.

"Help!"

Ingeborg's cry echoed off the white tiled walls of the large windowless room and filled the long, wide corridor of the clinic. The ward for disturbed patients who had been prescribed long baths contained seven grey-painted bathtubs along the outer wall, a row of washbasins along the other, and a lone, freestanding lavatory in the middle of the floor, on which a patient was sitting with her head in her hands.

"Help!" cried Ingeborg, who was lying in the bathtub in the far corner, under an unbleached burlap bath cover.

Ingeborg was kicking to free herself, causing water to squirt out of the opening at the foot of the bath cover. The previous night's opium treatment and the long bath had not succeeded in calming her down. She had an ice-cold bath compress on her head. Her hair had slid out of its bun and was hanging in wet clumps around her face and neck. The rough woman from the cleansing bath the previous day was pacing the floor and shaking her fist in Ingeborg's direction.

"Nothing good ever comes of a clenched fist," said the patient on the lavatory.

"Sofia, don't meddle in things that have nothing to do with you," said the orderly, who resembled a docker.

Sofia's medical history showed no mental illness in the family. She had a quiet, kind disposition and no abusive habits. She would often talk to the staff with regret about her two daughters, aged ten and twelve, who now had to take care of the housekeeping while their father tried to scrape together enough to put bread on the table in their croft. Sofia had been a patient at Restad for six months, but her oppressive headaches were not easing and seemed rather to be getting more intense. Her village doctor had thought at first she was pregnant, but when the nausea did not go away and she began forgetting things and losing her balance, he had sent her here for psychiatric treatment. Sofia was a Category III patient; in other words, the poor relief system covered her statutory care fees of just over a krona per day.

"Help!" cried Ingeborg again, shaking her head and causing the bath compress to fall to the floor.

"Sit still, woman!"

Leaning against the edge of the bathtub, the orderly slowly bent forward, wearily picked up the bath compress and put it back on Ingeborg's head, which was protruding through the round hole at the top end of the bath cover. Her plump, pasty face turned slightly pink from the exertion. When she saw a nurse appear at the entrance to the ward, she stood to attention. The nurse's clogs clattered on the marble floor as she walked over to the stove with its steaming copper pan. She poured some of the hot water into a pail and approached Ingeborg.

"Don't kill me!" cried Ingeborg, who raised her head to meet the nurse's eyes but was blinded by the harsh white light.

The three children had followed her when she moved the copper washtub from the hall into the bedroom. Ingeborg took the eldest first. She forced Tor's head down into the water. It was a hard thing to do, but necessary. Completely necessary. Tor offered no real resistance. Efraim put up more of a fight. Much more. Then, lastly, she took Lucia. When Ingeborg had finished, she lifted up the children's heads to make sure they were dead. Then she went and sat by the kitchen window.

The nurse crouched at the head of the bathtub and loosened the drawstring around Ingeborg's neck so that it was no longer chafing against her skin.

"Good afternoon, Mrs Andersson. I'm Sister Agnes. May I call you Ingeborg?"

Ingeborg reached out of the water, placed her hands on the coarse hemp cloth covering her body, and pulled herself up to a sitting position.

"Don't kill me!" she repeated, her eyes darting around.

Her parched, bluish skin was pulled tight around her knuckles. Her fingers were wrinkled. The previous day's encounter with the scrubbing brush had left red stripes on her back.

"Of course you are not going to die," replied Sister Agnes, stroking Ingeborg's hair. "We only want what is best for you."

The nurse felt the water, which had grown cold despite several top-ups with hot water in the course of the day.

"How long has Mrs Andersson been lying here?" asked Sister Agnes, turning to the orderly.

"Just seven hours."

Sister Agnes was about to pour the pail of hot water into the opening at the foot of the bath when she noticed that Ingeborg had done her business in the tub.

"How long has this patient been lying in her own excrement?" she inquired, but received no answer. "Get Mrs Andersson out of the bath at once and take her to the washroom. Once you have put her to bed, I need to speak to you in matron's office."

Neat and Tidy

"Good evening. My name is Sofia."

A thin woman in her thirties with wispy hair placed a shoebox containing a few personal possessions under the iron bed next to Ingeborg's. The beds were so close together that Ingeborg could feel the woman's warm breath. Ingeborg, who had been prescribed bed rest for the past few weeks, was tucked up and under supervision. The wide opening into the dormitory from the corridor allowed the staff to keep an eye on Ingeborg and the other patients without being too close. Bed rest was the predominant treatment at Restad and was considered especially beneficial for new arrivals.

Ingeborg was lying on her side, but a blade of straw was pricking her left shoulder. The room smelled of ammonia, but she didn't think it was her mattress that was urine-soiled. She had watched the staff empty it and change the straw the previous night. Ingeborg was thinking about Mother Selma, who had always used moss in the mattresses at home. Ingeborg's father would gather the moss in the woods in the autumn, and her mother would clean off the soil and roots and beat it with a stick before stuffing the mattresses.

In all there were eight beds with red woollen blankets in the dormitory of Ward 6A. Perhaps it was Sofia's mattress that smelled bad, thought Ingeborg, or somebody's bedpan. It couldn't be anyone's day clothes, because patients were not allowed to bring those into the dormitory. They had to be kept in the day room or the corridor.

"Don't worry about the Majoress, Ingeborg. That's what we call her, the woman in the baths. She's unpleasant, but Sister Agnes is kind," Sofia continued. "She has promised that I can show you my favourite spot by the river some day."

The dormitory had bright walls and big windows that locked with a special key. The wood of the window frames was reinforced with embedded iron bars, and the panes were so thick as to be unbreakable, according to the manufacturer.

A thin patient was dancing a silent dance in front of one of the windows. Illuminated from behind by the moonlight, her gracious, compulsive movements resembled shadow theatre.

"You were lucky to arrive in April, Ingeborg," said Sofia. "During the summer months, we don't have to go to bed until nine o'clock."

Another patient was hopping around the dormitory on one leg. Without warning, she flung herself headlong on the floor and started biting her forearms. She was about to attack the snoring patient in the bed next to her when the staff came running. They tried to restrain her with a belt, but she was too fat and managed to wriggle out. They then tried a harness, but the woman grabbed hold of the nurse's hair. In defending her head, the nurse involuntarily dropped the harness. The patient triumphantly held up a handful of hair. Eventually the staff managed to get her into the harness and secure it to the bed rail with a padlock. The woman thrashed so much that the whole bed rattled, but was unable to free herself.

"You'll soon get used to all the noise," whispered Sofia, crawling into the bed on Ingeborg's left. "Goodnight then."

Ingeborg heard her neighbour on the other side get up and take out the bedpan from under her bed, its metal scraping on the pine floorboards. The patient opposite sat up with her head in her hands and listened attentively to the tinkling.

"Good morning, ladies, it's six o'clock," said Sister Agnes, turning on the dormitory lamp with a special key.

Just as the prison bell controlled daily life at Växjö Women's Penitentiary, the time clock governed activities at Restad Hospital. This was a round clock in a black Bakelite case, about ten centimetres in diameter and half as thick. Sister Agnes carried it on a leather strap around her neck, along with all the hospital keys. Every morning, she would unlock its metal lid and enter her initials on the rotating cardboard disc. This enabled the hospital management to keep track of her and the other staff members around the clock.

"Oh my, the world is spinning today," said Sofia, forcing herself to smile as she tried to pull herself out of bed.

Ingeborg was already sitting up, and their knees collided in the tight space between the beds. A spot of blood had appeared on Ingeborg's pillow overnight, and Sofia's was soaked with sweat.

"My head is so sore," said Sofia, pointing to a spot just above her right temple. "It's a stabbing pain like toothache."

Sofia held her head between her hands, as if to make sure it was still there.

"You go on ahead, Ingeborg. Don't wait for me," she continued in a kind tone, without finishing her sentence.

Ingeborg, who had recovered after several weeks of bed rest, was first in the line of seven women behind Sister Agnes, who unlocked the dressing room.

Ingeborg took off her nightgown and washed carefully under her arms and breasts with soap and water. Sister Agnes trimmed her nails, so she would not harm herself, and helped her tie back her hair with a short ribbon. Ingeborg was not yet trusted with hairpins, but was often commended for her personal hygiene.

Maintaining a neat appearance, good personal hygiene and tidy surroundings was the beall and end-all of hospital life. The dormitory was cleaned and aired daily. On Fridays, all patients had a bath and a change of clothes. As a rule, the bedlinen was changed only once every three weeks unless the patient had soiled it.

After washing and dressing, Ingeborg and the other women on the ward for non-disturbed patients went to the refectory on the floor below, where they had breakfast together.

At seven o'clock, the food was collected from the kitchens and distributed according to the portion list for each ward. Once the trays and tin receptacles were in place, the patients were summoned to table. Today's breakfast menu was hash with herring. The rickety wooden chair, made by a patient, sagged when Ingeborg sat down in her assigned place opposite Sofia.

"Did you hear what happened last night?"

Sofia was whispering so that the duty staff would not hear her. The rules required several staff members to be present at mealtimes to maintain order, good manners and good behaviour.

"You must try to get a little nourishment," said the nurse.

Skinny Sofia had been served a boiled egg today, but was just sitting there with her hands in her lap, contemplating this delicacy. The nurse tried to spoon-feed her, but cajoling had no effect, and Sofia kept her mouth tightly closed.

"If you don't eat, we shall have to force-feed you."

Sofia immediately poked at a piece of herring in her hash and pretended to look interested. She didn't want the staff sticking that long probe down through her nostril again. Last time they had to hold her down on her back until it reached her stomach.

"Did you hear what happened?" repeated Sofia as the nurse moved on. "Some poor woman fell from the third floor trying to escape."

"Never!" exclaimed Ingeborg, eyeing Sofia's boiled egg.

Ingeborg had gained a couple of kilos since arriving at the hospital. The staff thought she was too fond of her food and were trying to make her cut down.

"The woman broke her neck when she hit the ground and died on the spot," Sofia went on, her voice trembling. "It's terrible."

"Never!" Ingeborg repeated, stealing another glance at Sofia's boiled egg.

She thought it would be a shame if such a nice egg went to waste. Sofia noticed her covetous gaze and pushed the egg cup over to Ingeborg's side of the table when the nurse wasn't looking.

"Thank you," said Ingeborg, quickly stuffing the soft-boiled egg into her mouth.

Egg yolk trickled out of the corner of Ingeborg's mouth as she chewed, and the string of yellow liquid rapidly solidified. Sofia gulped and held her hand to her mouth. No-one was allowed to leave the table until everyone had finished eating, but Sofia could hold out no longer. She raised her hand and asked to be escorted to the lavatory immediately.

"Before I have an accident," she pleaded.

Sister Agnes nodded and accompanied Sofia out into the corridor. When they reached the lavatory, she opened the door and let go of Sofia's hand.

"Can you manage by yourself now, Sofia?" asked Sister Agnes.

"I think so," replied Sofia, holding on to the wall for support.

She proceeded into the lavatory, taking short, strutting steps on her stiff legs and trying to avoid the puddles on the floor, so that her cloth shoes would not absorb the urine and bring it back into the room with her.

The lavatory was mopped down daily, but many of the patients did not know that they had to pull the chain to flush the toilet. Others would try to flush cloth sanitary towels down the drain, causing blockages. A normal toilet could not accommodate much cloth above the water trap, but the hospital had special toilets designed to prevent patients from reaching in and touching their own waste. The water trap was located deep below the floor and could be reached only with a special cleaning rod.

Sofia covered her mouth and nose with her hand. Finding a clean toilet in the far corner, she leaned over the rim and tried to vomit, but her stomach was empty. Again today, nothing came up apart from a little stomach acid that burned her throat. She had not eaten for ages. Sofia washed her hands and rinsed out her mouth before rejoining her fellow patients.

They were supposed to spend some quiet time socializing in the day room for half an hour before embarking on their assigned tasks and duties, but most of them just stood around like wallflowers, waiting for the workday to start — because the sooner it started, the sooner it would be over.

"No food may be removed from the refectory, as you well know, Mrs Andersson," one of the nurses scolded.

"Ingeborg brought the food for my sake," said Sofia. "Sister says I need to eat more."

Laundry

When the morning's social half-hour in the day room was over, the laundry crew assembled for the walk over to the washhouse, a small, free-standing building on the periphery of the hospital site. Sister Agnes went first, unlocking all the gates and doors along the way — a cumbersome procedure involving an unwieldy bunch of large keys.

Ingeborg walked alongside Sofia, holding on to her arm. The overseer had assigned them to the work crew responsible for laundry. From eight in the morning until six at night, with a two-hour dinner break from twelve till two, they knelt beside the river with their washboards and scrubbed away at stains, or laboured over the laundry tubs in the washhouse. Only the most trustworthy patients were allowed to work in the washhouse. It was meticulous work that required a certain knack and above all good hygiene. Freshly laundered sheets had to be stretched and pulled before being hung out to dry in the sun. Then all bedlinen and clothes had to be mangled and ironed. It was a position of honour. Ingeborg, Sofia and their fellow patients worked one hundred and fifty thousand man-days annually.

"Well, well, so the fine ladies have ended up in the madhouse too," said a familiar voice as they left the main building. "Patient number 1110 at your service."

When the man in the white undershirt and wide dungarees stood up straight and blew his nose into his hand, Ingeborg recognized Ivar the pauper, even though he must have gained at least twenty kilos since Liss's funeral three years previously.

Sister Agnes turned around and was about to tell Ivar to behave himself and stop harassing her ladies, but a young man leaning on a rake beat her to it.

"Leave the ladies alone," he said, raising his cap in greeting.

Sister Agnes nodded in reply, and the male patients went back to clearing dandelions from the lawn. A skinny simpleton was scampering around with a rake.

The small troop continued on its way, passing the staff quarters where Sister Agnes lived. The hospital management regarded nursing as a vocation, and female employees were not allowed to marry. Their ninety-hour work week left them with little leisure time anyway, so Sister Agnes found it convenient to live at her place of work.

As the women drew level with the gatehouse, the stench hit them. The drainpipe from the lavatories emptied into the adjacent stream. A charitable foundation had agreed to fund an extension of the outlet pipe, but construction was not yet under way.

"Catch!" shouted the gatekeeper's son to his playmate, preparing to throw a ball.

Ingeborg stopped and gazed at the boy running back and forth on the gravelled area in front of the gatehouse and pretending to be Sven Rydell, Sweden's top soccer player. He looked to be about the same age as Tor, and Ingeborg suddenly found herself short of breath.

"It's my turn to be Sven," replied his playmate, grabbing the homemade ball and running off.

Tor pursued him, straying dangerously close to the sewer outlet.

"Mind you don't fall in and drown!" Ingeborg wanted to shout, but was unable to utter a sound.

The boy had no chance of catching up and sat down cross-legged in the dirt, sulking. Just as Tor used to sit next to the loom at home, cutting strips for rag rugs. Although Tor never sulked.

The boy's friend had stopped running and was waving the ball around to tease him. One corner of the cloth had come loose and was flapping behind the ball like a comet's tail. Realizing eventually that he had lost his only teammate, he stopped fooling around and instead tried to push the dirty scrap of cloth back under the piece of string that held the ball together. This was difficult, because the gatekeeper had tied it so tight. He finally managed it, but got his forefinger caught under the string, which dug in and left a nasty red gash before he managed to free himself.

"There we are, good as new," he said sagely, putting the ball in his friend's lap. "We can both be Sven if you like."

The boys carried on pretending they were playing for Örgryte Idrottssällskap, the soccer team with three Sven Rydells, until the gatekeeper told them it was time to come in for something to eat. Just as Artur used to tell Tor.

"They're growing up so fast," said Sofia, smiling kindly at the gatekeeper.

"Thank you, Sofia. Is that a new friend you have with you?"

"Yes, this is Ingeborg," said Sofia, placing a hand on Ingeborg's shoulder.

"What a lovely name," replied the gatekeeper, nodding. "Do you have any children, Ingeborg?"

The Loom

"I didn't know any better, being so young," whispered Ingeborg to Sofia, scratching her head, as they left the steaming hot washhouse at the end of the workday.

Rising, eating, cleaning, bathing, working, resting; for everything there is a time, read the sign above the door.

Ingeborg looked at her chapped hands. She put a couple of the swollen fingers in her mouth and sucked on one of the cracks to dull the throbbing pain. The smell of soap lingered in the rainy air as the patients lined up outside the brick building. Ingeborg clasped her hands over her jute apron. The back of her neck tickled as a few drops of perspiration ran down her spine.

Ingeborg waited to be counted and checked off the list of living patients. The doctor made a round to check that none of them had drowned themselves in the river or stolen a table knife and slit their throat in the lavatory. Accidents were rare in this world governed by time clocks, keys and bath covers, but occasionally the staff failed to keep their patients under close enough supervision.

"Mother threw me a stick as I jumped on the hay wagon," Ingeborg continued in a low voice. "I must have only been five or six, and I couldn't catch it. It hurt as it hit my shin, but I soon forgot about it. I was just so happy that Mother wanted to play with me. She never usually played with us. So I threw the stick back. I didn't know any better."

Ingeborg fell silent as the doctor approached and stood right in front of her, holding the incontinence register. He kept a statistical record of each patient's relationship to their bodily secretions. A one meant they could not control their bladder. A two meant they could not control their bowels. A three meant they soiled things with their urine or feces. A four meant they consumed it.

The doctor nodded approvingly as he checked off Ingeborg and Sofia. Thanks to patients like them, the incontinence figures could be kept in check. Most patients found themselves in the first category at some point, but right now his only concern was a three: a man who was soiling walls and bedlinen. Fortunately the man had typhoid and could be kept locked up on account of the infection risk.

"This year the incontinence rate among female patients is only six percent, down by a whole percentage point since last year," the doctor noted with satisfaction as he moved on to the next row.

"Mother came running toward me," said Ingeborg, resuming her story. "She didn't want to play. Instead, she grabbed me by the shoulders, shook me and screamed that she had given birth to me for her sins. I only wanted to play, Sofia. I didn't know any better."

"Yes, to think of everything we had to go through before life brought the two of us together," said Sofia, patting Ingeborg's shoulder.

After the doctor's round, Sister Agnes gathered together those capable of learning a handicraft to keep them occupied once the workday was over. The men made baskets or brushes and did woodwork. The women knitted and crocheted with coarse yarn. Occupational therapy was an important tool in the fight against mental illness, and Dr Ottosson, the chief physician, was so convinced of the health benefits to patients that he had sent Sister Agnes to Germany on a three-week study visit. On her return, she had been tasked with setting up a weaving studio, which was to be opened today.

Ingeborg and Sofia followed Sister Agnes across the courtyard into the stairwell of the main building and up to the third floor. Sofia was puffing and panting and had to take a rest as soon as they reached the first landing.

"Hold on to the rope," suggested Ingeborg, pointing to the thick rope attached to the wall of the spiral staircase and taking Sofia's hand. It felt as if they were inside a stone cylinder. The weaving studio was at the top on the right, where a nurse was waiting for them in the open doorway. She was handing out old patient uniforms, which had to be torn into strips and woven into pale blue rag rugs. The rain was bucketing down and lashing the large windows. A draught from the crevices whistled around the nurse's bare arms and legs.

"Aren't you cold, sister?" inquired Sofia. "Would you like to borrow my cardigan?"

"Thank you, Sofia. That's kind of you, but there's no need. I'll soon warm up, I'm sure."

The huge room with its high ceiling echoed as Ingeborg crossed the threshold. In front of each uncurtained window stood a brand new floor loom. Ingeborg looked around the room and counted eight looms in all. She walked over to the loom nearest the door and touched the pale wood that had not yet darkened with time. Then she eased herself into the seat, gently placed her hands on the wooden frame, and traced the warp threads back and forth with her right forefinger. She stroked the shuttle and gingerly nudged the pedals with one foot. The scent of freshly sawn pine took her back in time, to another place, another world. Seven years ago now. An eternity.

"Come on, up you get!" Artur had said, sticking his head around the bedroom door on the morning after their wedding.

Ingeborg was still lazing in the bed while Artur washed the dishes after breakfast.

"You haven't had your morning gift yet," her husband went on.

Half an hour later, they were walking across the farmyard to the woodworking shed, where scraps of bark were flying as Artur's brother sharpened fence posts.

"Good morning," said Holger, wiping his brow with his forearm. "So, the happy couple are awake at last."

"We've been awake a good while, I'll have you know," said Artur.

"I'm sure you have," replied Holger, laughing. "I'm only teasing."

"Thank you so much for the lovely wooden frames you carved for us," said Ingeborg, patting her brother-in-law on the shoulder.

"They'll be nice for photographs of the children when they arrive," said Holger.

"Three of them! I can never imagine us having so many children," Ingeborg replied, turning to her husband. "What was it you wanted to show me?"

"Guess," said Artur, pointing to a tarpaulin in the corner.

"A vehicle?"

"Better than that," replied Artur, removing the cover from the square contraption.

"A beautiful loom for me!" Ingeborg exclaimed. "But it's much too nice to stand out here and be ruined. You must take it indoors."

"I'm not sure we have room for it," said Artur rhetorically, before asking his brother to help carry it.

"There's nothing much in the parlour," said Ingeborg, running on ahead to look for a suitable spot in the house.

"Good morning, boys, up and about already?" inquired Farmor as she emptied a washbasin of soapy water into the slush bucket outside the cottage. "Where are you going with that monstrosity?"

"The lady of the house wants the loom in the parlour," explained Holger.

"Are you out of your minds?"

"If Ingeborg wants the loom in the parlour, we'll put the loom in the parlour," Artur retorted.

Ingeborg smiled at the memory. Her eyes twinkled.

"Do you like weaving, Ingeborg?" asked Sister Agnes, who had stolen up behind her.

Taken by surprise, Ingeborg quickly pulled her hands away from the warp.

"Yes," she replied after a moment. "I like weaving very much."

Ingeborg is skilful and industrious, Sister Agnes noted carefully on her chart at the end of the workday.

Trional

Ingeborg was awakened by a cold breeze sweeping through the ward. The cotton curtain was billowing like a hot-air balloon preparing for take-off, before collapsing back on the empty bed in front of the window, as if the propane had suddenly run out.

"The patient has never exhibited any aggressive tendencies before," said the matron. "It must be a side effect of the medication."

Ingeborg noticed that her neighbour in the bed opposite was missing, and realized it must have been her that broke the window and attacked the night nurse with a glass shard.

The matron flipped through the patient's weight chart, medication chart, menstruation chart and incontinence chart until she found the chart she was looking for.

"See?" she went on, showing Dr Ottosson the record of incidents.

The chief physician looked at the sheet of graph paper containing not a single cross, and nodded. Perhaps the night nurse was not guilty of professional negligence. Perhaps he should let her keep her job. But accidents were unsettling for staff and patients alike, not to mention board members and patients' families. So far this year, he had only had to report one near miss. This latest incident would also have to be included in the hospital's annual report. That was bad, very bad.

"We don't yet know how many stitches the night nurse needed," continued the matron.

In normal circumstances, the matron and the chief physician would not be around so early. The staff on the night shift usually handed over the time clock to the day shift at six in the morning.

"The night nurse managed to overpower her, but by then the damage had been done. The patient has now been given trional and transferred to the ward for disturbed patients. The staff have tied her to the iron bars of the bed in case she is still agitated when she wakes up."

The matron held her hand over her mouth and nose, struggling to breathe steadily and not lose control. She looked ready to burst into tears at any moment. She blew a couple of stray strands of hair off her forehead. They fell straight back into her eyes, and she pushed them back with two damp fingers, as if trying to stick them to her scalp. The chief physician remained silent. Having a nurse admitted to the emergency room did not look good at all.

"There was no negligence involved," insisted the matron. "The night nurse is one of my best. No-one could have foreseen this situation."

Perhaps I need to review the matron's suitability instead, thought Dr Ottosson. It might be unfortunate to inflict further punishment on the night nurse when God had already withdrawn his protective hand from her. Perhaps it would be unfair to punish her twice over.

"The windows are meant to be unbreakable, according to the manufacturer!"

Dr Ottosson raised his hand and made a hushing noise to calm the matron down. It looked as though he was patting a dog in mid-air. Meanwhile, he gathered the glass shards into a pile with his foot and clicked his fingers in the direction of the cleaner, who immediately came running to sweep up.

Ingeborg was sobbing and moaning, but no-one was paying her any attention this morning.

"Will the night nurse dare come back to work after this?" asked the chief physician at last. "Her face has been completely disfigured."

"Her work means everything to her. We are her family. She has no-one apart from us. If she loses her job, she will end up in the poorhouse. Please be compassionate, Dr Ottosson," implored the matron, clasping her hands.

Ingeborg was chewing on the edge of the sheet. Her hands were stuck inside a pair of flat, dark brown mittens made of stiff leather. She could not move her fingers, much less scratch her head. She had a lipoma in the middle of her skull that she could not leave alone. Blood from it had clotted in her hair during the night, forming two matted clumps that had left brown stains on the pillowcase. The movable lump of fatty tissue just under the skin had grown so large that it needed surgery. The doctor explained that he would make a small incision with a scalpel over the lump so it could be removed from the sac that enclosed it.

"It's a simple operation," he assured Ingeborg.

But Ingeborg didn't want an operation. She wanted to rip a hole in her skin and remove the fatty cyst herself. She wanted to continue sucking her blood red fingers that tasted of iron, but the leather mittens were in the way, and her forefinger was growing numb, as though someone was sticking pins in its tip. The gloves were secured with a round padlock at the wrist, known as an idiot lock. An idiot-proof lock for idiots. Ingeborg fell asleep and dreamed about her parents.

"Light the stove and put the coffee on," said her father, donning his work trousers.

In her dream, he resembled Dr Goldkuhl, and Mother Selma had polio. Her father was going out to milk the cows, but had to have coffee first. Just a cup on its own. Ingeborg was hurrying but couldn't get the fire to light. She took a piece of newspaper, placed it under the firewood and blew gently. Thick black smoke welled up. She had forgotten to open the damper. A glowing coal landed on the floor. The fire spread rapidly, and the rag rugs in the bedroom turned to ash as the raging flames consumed everything in their path. They licked the floor and wound themselves like snakes around the wooden legs of Mother Selma's bed. Ingeborg's father tried to help his wife out of the house, but polio had robbed her of the use of her legs. She could not stand up, let alone walk, and could not feel the heat. Mother was on fire, and it was Ingeborg's fault.

Mother's Day

Ingeborg and Sofia walked out into the gardens, where preparations were under way for a party for patients, staff and employees' families. Sofia picked an armful of bleeding heart from the round flowerbed. The sun was shining through the cobweb between two stems. She buried her heavy head in the flowers and inhaled their scent as deeply as she could, as if they might cure the throbbing pain in her temples. Or as if she knew deep down that this was the last summer when she would be able to tie bunches of flowers for the clay vases on the long table that the gatekeeper had set up outside the main building.

Ingeborg walked slowly toward the kitchen. She stopped on the threshold to dissect the pink and white pendant flower that Sofia had given her, unpicking layer upon layer, thread upon thread. The flower reminded her of a Russian doll full of surprises.

"Don't just stand there dreaming, Ingeborg. Only a few minutes left! Run and feed this swill to the pigs right away!" cried the cook, hurrying across the chequered floor with a bucket. "And don't stop for a chat with everyone you see. The guests will be here any minute now."

The cook handed Ingeborg the bucket containing the pig swill and gave her a shove in the back to make her hurry up. Then she hastened back to the potatoes she was boiling in a copper pan on the built-in stove.

Ingeborg walked across the courtyard. The gatekeeper waved, but she was too preoccupied with the task in hand to notice. She carried on to the barn and opened the iron latch on the door. She was about to throw the swill to the pigs when she heard someone crying on the other side of the feed box.

"What are you doing here?" asked Ingeborg, looking down into the pen of the newborn calf, where the hospital's oldest patient was sitting on a bed of straw, rocking back and forth, her hand white with froth.

Visually impaired and hard of hearing, the old woman did not notice Ingeborg opening the feed box.

"He's hungry, my brother," she sobbed to herself.

Ingeborg sat down beside the old woman, took her shrivelled hand in her own and gently dried it with her handkerchief. The woman had cut up her patient uniform and sewn the scraps back together with blanket stitch.

"They are not feeding him. Look, he is suckling," she said, reaching out toward the calf.

"The farmhand just brought him a big pail of warm milk. I saw him bringing it," said Ingeborg. "Now he is probably just tired and needs to sleep off his food."

"I must have had another crazy turn," said the old woman, looking up at Ingeborg. "May is always such a hard month. That was when it happened."

"We all have crazy turns at one time or another," said Ingeborg. "Father killed my brother with a ten-inch knife. He sacrificed his only son, like Abraham in the book of Exodus. Father was locked up in Malmö castle after that. Seven years' hard labour and then the madhouse in the same town. Just like me."

"Come on, let's go and have something to eat," said Ingeborg, helping the old woman to her feet.

1. The flag of Sweden is to be raised on the flagpole of the house. 2. Mother is to be greeted in the morning with a song by the children. 3. Before rising, she is to be brought coffee and bread; preferably bread baked by the children themselves. She is to be honoured with flowers and a small gift. 4. She is to be allowed rest and freedom from all housework, as far as possible. The children are to help out around the house as much as they can: cleaning, preparing food, and washing dishes. 5. At afternoon coffee or in the evening, a small ceremony is to be held, in which the father of the house participates. Something beautiful is to be read aloud, and heartfelt thanks expressed to Mother, who is the force that keeps the home together. 6. Absent children are to send Mother a greeting by letter or telegram.

Sofia shook her head, asking herself what the hospital management were thinking, having a Mother's Day celebration at an institution for unhappy and childless mothers. Sofia tried to conceal the notice on the table before Ingeborg sat down, but she had already seen it.

"I was mentally ill when it happened," said Ingeborg.

"I know," said Sofia.

"My crime troubled me sorely at first, but it's better now. The hardest time was between February and Midsummer of 1928. Lucia was only two months old when it started. I felt so tired and apathetic. I was lethargic, and all I wanted to do was lie down. Yes, it was sinful, but it wasn't my intention to make the children suffer for my sins."

Ingeborg looked upset. Her gaze wandered between Sofia and her hands in her lap.

"Of course it wasn't," said Sofia, taking Ingeborg's hand in her own.

"I couldn't make sense of myself. I just felt constrained. I couldn't do anything around the house, although I knew exactly what needed doing. And I was scared of other people! Although I knew they were nothing to be scared of."

"To think of everything we had to go through before life brought the two of us together," said Sofia, stroking Ingeborg's cheek.

"I was such a wretch when I arrived in prison," Ingeborg went on. "Now I feel better. Almost like my old self. The illness probably won't come back now. When I'm this well, surely it can't come back, can it, Sofia?"

"It won't do that, Ingeborg. You are well now. Dr Ottosson says it's only a matter of time until you're allowed to go home."

"Artur doesn't want me back."

"Why do you say that, Ingeborg? He has forgiven you."

"So he says. But I don't believe he can forgive me, Sofia. Even if he wanted to."

Birthday

"Are you allowed flowers in the ward, do you think?"

Mother Selma looked uneasily around the day room for someone to ask. It was one o'clock in the afternoon of June 14, 1930, Ingeborg's twenty-ninth birthday. She had just had dinner. The smell of disinfectant and freshly polished floors mixed with that of blood bread and pork stew. From the corridor came the clatter of dishes as the nurses loaded them onto large serving trolleys to be taken back to the kitchen through the culvert.

This was the first time Selma had visited her daughter in the hospital, and she was concerned to do everything right. She carefully read the instructions pinned to the wallpaper in the hallway:

Visitors must not give patients anything other than periodicals and edible items. Permission to give a patient anything else must be obtained from the matrons. The hospital is not liable for any valuables brought to the ward by patients and not deposited with the matrons for safekeeping. Giving weapons or sharp objects to patients is a criminal offence, punishable by a fine of up to 1,000 kronor or imprisonment under chapter 8, section 53, of the Penal Code. The Director.

"Perhaps it would be best to ask matron about the flowers anyway?" Selma went on, glancing at the violets before getting up from the table.

"They must surely allow you something to cheer you up on your birthday! These flowers smell so lovely and are not poisonous. But I can't see a vase anywhere. I should have brought a jar. How could I forget? Silly me!"

Mother Selma walked slowly toward the doorway and peeked cautiously out into the corridor.

"That nurse was most helpful, I'll say," said Selma when she returned a short while later with a triumphant smile on her face and a zinc mug filled with water.

"How nice," said Ingeborg.

"The nurse said the flowers can stay in the day room, where all the patients can enjoy them."

"Sister Agnes is awfully nice," said Ingeborg, picking at the lace edge of the white tablecloth embellished with yellow and deep pink roses in cross-stitch.

Just then the old woman came by and deposited her bedpan right in the middle of the table.

"I think you're in the wrong place," said Selma, barely able to contain her laughter.

"Don't go scaring Ingeborg's mother away, now," said Sister Agnes, who had come running to the rescue. "Come on, let's go to the lavatory instead."

"I must have had another crazy turn," said the old woman.

"That's all right," said Ingeborg.

"Do they feed you well?" asked Selma, turning back to her daughter.

"I can't complain. Can't you see how plump I've grown since I arrived here?"

"Yes, you're looking nice and round! Do you get dessert too?"

"Every day. Today it was tapioca."

"Then you'll have two desserts today," said Selma, producing a thermos flask and two cardamom buns from her basket. "Because now it's time for some after-dinner coffee."

Selma took out two china cups decorated with turquoise floral vines and poured a drop of cream into each of them.

"Hope the coffee hasn't gone cold."

Mother Selma, who had few teeth left in her upper jaw, dunked her bun in the coffee to make it easier to chew. As she raised it to her mouth, a piece broke off and landed in the cup. The hot coffee splashed onto her chin, and she quickly wiped it off before anyone noticed her bad manners. The soggy piece of bun sank to the bottom, and Selma tried to fish out the light brown mush with a teaspoon. When it did not cooperate, she stuck her forefinger into the lukewarm coffee and gently pushed the piece of bun onto the spoon. Then she inquired, with her mouth agape:

"Is that good?"

"Yes, that tastes *so* good, Mother!"

"You should see the rain we've had at home. I've never seen anything like it. The neighbour is going to lose all his hay. It's lying in the meadows and rotting. He's too impatient, you see. Always has to be first out. But this year he learned his lesson. Your father didn't mow until yesterday. And you should have seen how much grass there was! The whole village came by to help build drying racks. Even the neighbour pitched in, for that matter. He's not workshy, I must say, but he's too sure of himself. When your father and brother set about putting up the posts and wires for the drying racks, that wasn't good enough for him, you know. In the end your brother got so irritated that he swore and told the man to 'clear off home and let my father and me work in peace'. Yes, those were his very words. Then we all had a good laugh, I can tell you. Tomorrow they're going to tackle the neighbour's fields, even though it's Sunday. The pastor can say whatever he likes, your father says."

Mother Selma fell silent for a moment to catch her breath.

"Sister Agnes says you help out in the kitchen and peel potatoes," she went on.

"Yes, but usually I work in the laundry," said Ingeborg. "It's nice."

"Yes, she told me that too, the nurse did. She said you work hard. That's good to hear. You should never be afraid of hard work," said Selma, before changing the subject. "I see you've got a fire extinguisher here. That's a good thing."

Selma pointed to a copper bucket with iron feet, a pump and a fabric hose in the corner of the day room. She was about to continue, but stopped herself and fell silent for a moment, as if deciding whether to mention the recent accident at home.

"The neighbour's barn burned down last Sunday."

"Never!" said Ingeborg. "I had a horrible nightmare about that."

"The thunderstorm struck at half past four in the morning. I had just got up and put the coffee on. At first I thought it was the house on fire. Your father pulled on his trousers as fast as he could and dashed over there in his clogs. He didn't even stop to put his boots on, but they still didn't manage to get the animals out. The cows were grazing in the pasture, of course, but all the young stock perished in the flames. The fire brigade didn't arrive until the entire hayloft had burned to the ground. They were lucky it wasn't the house. The old lady would never have got out in time. Old people shouldn't keep livestock, I've always said. Well, I'll have to leave soon if I'm going to catch the train home."

Well-behaved patients were allowed to take a half-hour walk unsupervised, so Ingeborg accompanied her mother for part of the way. They walked through the grove to the lookout point, where they watched the swans feeding their cygnets down by the jetty at the bathing area, Sofia's favourite spot by the river. When it was time for her to go and catch the bus back to the station, Selma extended her hand to say goodbye. She hesitated for a moment and then said, with downcast eye:

"What you don't know can't hurt you, but I think you have a right to know. We had a letter the other day. I don't want to spoil your birthday, but Dr Goldkuhl has died. On the tenth of May. He survived his wife by only six months."

Leave of Absence

"You know what, Ingeborg? Today I feel happy!" said Sofia. "I'm happy because I woke up this morning to live another day. Yes, that's why I'm happy!"

An explanation had finally been found for Sofia's fatigue, oppressive headaches, lack of appetite and waddling gait. Sofia had never been insane. It was cancer. And now she was too exhausted to move back home or to another hospital.

Ingeborg was happy too. Her toothache had gone away, and she had slept well, without medication, for the past few nights. The previous week she had attended the dental clinic to have a wisdom tooth extracted. She had only had to pay a few kronor, and the institution, the state or a charity — she wasn't sure which — had paid the rest. Now she felt ready and willing, tidy and respectable, and almost as cheerful and eager as that time when she and Artur went to the Jubilee Exhibition in Gothenburg. Although it was ages since she had heard from her husband.

Ingeborg and Sofia waited in the day room. Their application for leave of absence had been granted, and when Sister Agnes appeared, the three of them went downstairs together and out into the gardens. Sister Agnes and Ingeborg helped to support Sofia, taking one arm each.

A black Scania-Vabis bus, with its route displayed on the side in large white lettering, like a go-faster stripe, pulled up at the bus stop on the road outside the hospital. Ingeborg and Sofia boarded and sat in one of the front seats so they could look out through the large rectangular windscreen. Sister Agnes paid the conductor.

Fifteen minutes later, the bus arrived at Vänersborg station, just as the train had done that evening almost two years previously. This was the first time Ingeborg had visited the town since. Then it had been dark and cold. Now it was just cold. Ingeborg pulled her coat more tightly around her and wondered whether it had been such a good idea to take a trip into town in the middle of winter. She looked down to avoid seeing the Penitentiary on the hill opposite the station. Overlooking the entire neighbourhood, it seemed to be watching the inhabitants' every move.

The three women from Restad struggled up the hill, past the alley leading to the prison, to one of the town's cafés. Sister Agnes had suggested they spend the afternoon over a cup of coffee and a couple of almond muffins. Ingeborg's galoshes — the same galoshes as back then — seemed to have a momentum of their own. The boa grew tight at her neck, and she was breathing heavily, panting. A man riding a kicksled came over the crest of the hill. The sun had been beating down on the slope, and as the man drew level with Ingeborg, one of the runners cut through the thin ice to the pavement beneath, causing sparks to fly. Ingeborg shuddered, thinking it sounded like a dentist's drill slipping.

"What can I get you, ladies?" inquired a waitress in a long white apron with frills on the shoulder straps.

Sister Agnes ordered for all three of them, and when the girl had finished taking down the order and looked up from her notepad, she placed her hand on Ingeborg's shoulder and exclaimed in astonishment:

"It's Mrs Andersson, isn't it?"

Ingeborg looked up into a pair of familiar blue eyes.

The nurserymaid had been noisily washing dishes in the kitchen on the morning of March 11, 1928. Mother Selma had poured a drop of milk into her freshly brewed coffee and was holding her saucer with three fingers, blowing gently on the coffee so it wouldn't scald her. Efraim had crawled up on her lap, and she was rocking Lucia's cradle with her foot. The beater of the loom in the parlour was silent. Ingeborg's hands were resting on the warp.

"Come on, let's go and join the others," said Tor, but Ingeborg sat motionless in her nightgown.

Once Lucia had fallen asleep, Selma carried the cradle back into the parlour. Ingeborg's mother had come over from the next village to help her eldest son with the funeral arrangements. They had been to Herrljunga to buy a coffin for sixty kronor, and had cycled around delivering funeral invitations to friends and family, neighbours and acquaintances. They had cut twenty-six sheaves of chaff for the mortuary in the barn, its walls draped with white sheets. After a few days of fever, palpitations and severe abdominal pain, Liss had passed away. Now he was at rest with his hands folded in an open coffin surrounded by spruce twigs.

"I can't fathom it. Only the other day, we were sitting here eating fried pork with onion sauce, and now he's gone," said the nurserymaid, clutching her handkerchief convulsively.

She held it to her nose and wiped hard. The teardrops made the fabric transparent. Her face was swollen, her nose chapped and red like Liss's wound.

"He died of blood poisoning. And there we were, thinking it was an upset stomach," the nurserymaid continued, banging her forehead with her clenched fist.

Mother Selma patted the girl on the shoulder and went over to the stove to get another cup of coffee.

"Don't you recognize me, Mrs Andersson?" asked the waitress when Ingeborg made no reply.

"It's been such a long time."

Ingeborg stared at the cornflower blue chintz sofa, gently stroking the soft upholstery back and forth, back and forth.

"I'm sorry for your loss," said the girl, putting the coffee on the house. "I read about the tragedy in the newspaper."

"Thank you, Astrid."

Ingeborg looked up at the girl. Her cheek was twitching slightly.

"You must promise me you'll come back soon, Mrs Ingeborg, so I can introduce you to my son."

"I didn't know. That's nice."

"Liss is three years old already. He's the spitting image of his father. Every bit as playful and full of mischief. You would like him, Mrs Ingeborg. You were like a sister to his father."

Farewell

On the south-facing slope, a lone coltsfoot was a bright spot among the dry remnants of last year's grass. Ingeborg almost tripped over the tuft as she prepared to jump the embankment bordering the ditch. Sister Agnes took her hand, and they walked arm in arm the rest of the way across the field, in slush up to their ankles.

On Sundays and holy days, church services were held at Restad Hospital. According to section thirteen of the hospital rules, these services were *to be attended by those patients who might derive benefit and edification from so doing, and by as many members of hospital staff as deemed necessary*. No such rules applied to funerals at the hospital. Sister Agnes and Ingeborg were the only guests in attendance.

Please bring condolences only, they had written on Liss's funeral invitations, but the table was still laden with dishes and jugs. There had been a steady stream of neighbours, relatives and friends bringing sandwiches and cookies as a token of sympathy.

"What are we going to do with all this food?" sighed Mother Selma to the nurserymaid as they helped serve morning coffee to the funeral guests.

"It will get eaten up, you'll see. After the service and the burial, everyone is sure to be hungry again," said the pastor, thanking her for the excellent cookies. "Did you bake them yourself, Selma?"

"You think so, pastor? They turned out such odd shapes this time! But if you can bear to eat them, pastor, please tuck in."

The driver picked up the reins, and the steel wire between the wooden, iron-clad rear wheels jerked as the hearse moved slowly off across the spruce twigs that had been strewn on the farm road. The horse's hooves clattered against the cobbles on Liss's final journey. Just a few days earlier, he had been sitting in the driving seat himself, laughing and shouting and encouraging the horse. Now he lay washed and shrouded in a coffin beneath a black canopy, in a hearse bound for the church. From its roof, a velvet valance billowed, with three white fringes on the long side and one on the short side. A wreath of roses hung from one of the white crosses atop the hearse. A silk sash inscribed with Astrid's name fluttered in the wind. Wearing a light-coloured coat and a round straw hat, she walked falteringly alongside Ingeborg behind the squeaky vehicle. Artur walked with them, holding his wife's arm.

In the graveyard on the far side of the field stood hundreds of black cast-iron crosses, row on row. The crosses bore no names, merely a number prefixed with M for male patients and K for females. Ingeborg caught sight of a new cross farthest to the right, numbered M1110, with a couple of frozen white lilies lying at its foot. Easter lilies. She bent down to sniff them, but the frost had killed the scent.

"Patient number 1110 at your service."

"Yes, that's what he used to say," said Sister Agnes. "Ivar's time on earth came to an end last week. He died of dysentery."

Ingeborg had chosen white lilies for the children's funeral too. Easter lilies. Three small wreaths of shiny green leaves and white lilies. One for Tor, one for Efraim and one for Lucia.

The young hospital chaplain came walking briskly toward them, holding out his hand.

"Good afternoon," he said breathlessly, interrupting Ingeborg's thoughts. "Sorry I'm late."

Ingeborg and Sister Agnes curtsied. The chaplain went over to Sofia's cross and began his homily. He spoke of joy and thankfulness, of everything Sofia had achieved during her lifetime in the service of the Lord. And he spoke of Sofia's humility, of how she would never accept any praise.

"Therefore I will not say what I would otherwise wish to say. For I am certain that Sofia has become no less humble since she joined her Heavenly Father, and therefore she would not wish to hear any praise from us gathered here today. What she would wish is that we should thank God for the grace and power He gave her for the sake of Our Lord Jesus Christ. Let us end by singing hymn number 31."

Fair are the meadows,

> Fairer still the woodlands,
> Robed in the blooming garb of spring.
> Jesus is fairer, Jesus is purer,
> Who makes the woeful heart to sing.[4]

"Perhaps they will bury me out here too," said Ingeborg when the chaplain had finished speaking and rushed off to his next duty. "Maybe I should just stay on until that time comes?"

"But you have family, Ingeborg," replied Sister Agnes. "You're not going to end up here!"

"Sofia had family too," said Ingeborg.

Sofia's husband could not afford to have his wife's body brought back to their village. He could not even afford to attend the funeral at the hospital. He did not earn enough from his croft to pay for a ticket to Vänersborg and back. A couple of hours' journey, ninety kilometres. Sofia's daughters were not able to say goodbye to their mother.

Just as Ingeborg had not been able to say goodbye to her daughter Lucia. Ingeborg was thinking about her children. About Tor and Efraim. She wondered if anyone had read her last words to them at the funeral, the words inscribed on the white wreath sashes: *Forgive me.*

"Do you think I'll be able to go home soon, Sister Agnes?" asked Ingeborg after a while. "Time is passing quickly, but I'm missing home now."

"Of course you will. And if you have insomnia, you can always come back here, I promise," said Sister Agnes.

"The Almighty is kind," said Ingeborg, placing her funeral bouquet on the frozen ground in front of cross number K603 and whispering:

"To think of everything we had to go through before life brought the two of us together, Sofia."

Växjö, April 24, 1930

Dear Mr Andersson,

Owing to a prolonged illness and other circumstances, I am only now in a position to reply to your letter. As you will be aware, Ingeborg is now in Vänersborg; it is uncertain when she may be discharged, but you must bear in mind that she has been absolved of any responsibility for her act by a Swedish court, on the grounds that she was mentally ill at the time the act was committed. It cannot therefore be claimed that she is responsible for the grave misfortune that has befallen you both. No court will accept such a claim as grounds for divorce.

If we are to discuss responsibility for the unfortunate incident, then it lies primarily with those around Ingeborg. It is unreasonable to allow a poor mother to remain so clearly unwell for such a long time without making any attempt to obtain help for her or even trying to ascertain the cause of her suffering.

You should visit Ingeborg and talk to her current doctor. You will then learn that her illness is such that a complete recovery certainly cannot be ruled out.

From the case documents, which the judge can show you, you can see that she was not pregnant, much less had given birth.

With my sincere sympathy and heartfelt best wishes to Ingeborg, of whom we all became very fond; she is an exceptionally sweet and kind woman.

Very truly yours,
H. Goldkuhl
Physician-in-Charge
Växjö Women's Penitentiary

Epilogue

For seventy years, no-one in my family talked about Tor, Efraim and Lucia. I was not even aware of their existence until my cousin mentioned the murders one day in July 1999. My cousin was an occupational therapist, and one of her patients had asked if she was related to Ingeborg Andersson, who had killed her three children on the morning of March 22, 1929.

Ingeborg was my maternal grandmother's sister. As a child, I went with my mother to visit her in various care homes in Ljung, Borås and Alingsås. She was the slightly overweight lady in the flowery dresses and ugly hats who used to scream for help. I didn't know she had been married and had three children: two boys and a little girl.

At the time of writing, Tor would have been ninety-four years old and Efraim ninety-two. Lucia, who was born the same year as my mother, would have turned ninety-one on December 13, 2018. They were my mother's cousins.

Ingeborg's story touched me so deeply that I could not deal with it. So, like everyone else in my family, I put it to one side. For fifteen years. I did exactly the same as the relatives I would condemn for their silence and their inability to talk about important matters. Now I realize this might have been their only way to keep going, to survive.

Tor, Efraim and Lucia were laid to rest in the family grave of their paternal grandparents in 1929, but the small rectangular stone with the inscription *Suffer little children to come unto me* was buried shortly after, and all photographs of the children were destroyed.

My story ends in 1930, when twenty-nine-year-old Ingeborg was a patient at Restad mental hospital. A year later, she was conditionally discharged for the first time and moved in with her parents. Ingeborg's brother Martin, eighteen years her senior and her designated guardian, wrote later that month to the chief physician at Restad:

> I beg to inform you that the conditionally discharged patient Ingeborg Maria Andersson, from Vesene, remains fit and well and is at work every day.

Similar reports were sent to the hospital on a monthly basis for the next five years. After her eventual divorce from Artur, Ingeborg was registered at her parents' address for census purposes. Ingeborg's father, August, who had suffered from depression all his life, died in July 1935 at the age of eighty-seven. Ingeborg looked after her sick mother, Selma, as best she could, but as time went on she became increasingly tired and reclusive. She complained of headaches and was worried her illness might be returning. Afraid that she might do something insane, she returned to Restad in February 1939 and asked to be treated as soon as possible. When the doctor brought up the subject of the dead children, she did not react at all. She was not grieving for them and did not harbour any remorse. She spoke of them with the utmost indifference. Ingeborg was to stay at the hospital for six months.

After the outbreak of the Second World War, Ingeborg was admitted to the hospital for six months a year on average, always at her own request. She had a hearty appetite and found it hard to hold back where food was concerned. During every hospital stay, she gained ten kilograms.

According to her medical records, Ingeborg was unconcerned by the political situation in Sweden. She had no financial worries, but cried over insomnia and strange thoughts. When her mother died in 1943 at the age of eighty, Ingeborg started working as housekeeper for her two unmarried cousins, Enok and Joel. One morning when the brothers woke up, Ingeborg was gone. They found her bicycle at the station. She had again caught the train to her safe place behind the institution's walls.

The next time Ingeborg was conditionally discharged, her siblings found her a job as a nanny in Kumla. She ran away from this job too, telling the staff at Restad that she could not bear the burden of responsibility. She was keen to get well and asked for electroconvulsive therapy to dispel her dark thoughts. After four electric shocks, she complained of headaches and discontinued the treatment.

My maternal grandfather, who was married to Ingeborg's sister Dagny, three years her senior, made a living by selling firewood to town residents during the war. Two years after the war ended, my grandparents and their five children moved into a new-build house with six rooms plus kitchen, electricity and indoor plumbing. At the age of eighteen, my mother had running water for the first time in her life. She shared a bedroom with her youngest sister. The draughty old cottage consisting of one room and a kitchen could finally be demolished.

My grandfather had made a bedroom and kitchen upstairs for Ingeborg, and in February 1948 she and her loom moved in. My mother, who by then was twenty-one, was the second eldest of her siblings. My aunts and uncles were aged between eight and twenty-three, and their memories of this time are mainly happy ones. They recall a slightly eccentric old lady who experienced strong mood swings and used to sit up late at night listening to the radio. She loved to win the twenty-five-öre pieces that others had wagered at casino, a card game.

She would add sugar lumps and blackcurrants to a five-litre wooden keg of small beer every day to turn it into fortified wine. She would wrap raw pork around her leg to alleviate the pain in her knee.

Ingeborg was a member of the village sewing circle and was known for her beautiful rag rugs. On Sundays she would cycle twenty-five kilometres to the outdoor church service in the neighbouring village. On Christmas Eve, she used to treat her new family to coffee, freshly baked buns and seven different kinds of cookies at half past five in the morning. Ingeborg stayed with my grandparents for almost twenty years.

In the mid-1950s, my grandmother had a heart attack. She never fully recovered, which may be why Ingeborg moved in with her brother, six years her senior, in a small apartment in the nearby community of Ljung. Her brother had remained a bachelor since his fiancée broke off their engagement one day in the spring of 1929. Possibly he blamed Ingeborg for this; in any event, he and Ingeborg did not get along. In 1968, after an absence of twenty years, Ingeborg was again admitted to Restad at her own request. Over the next four years, she was in and out of the psychiatric hospital nine times before the geriatric care system took over.

Big changes had taken place in mental health care during the twenty years that Ingeborg was living with my grandmother. Psychotropic medication was now in widespread use, and when Ingeborg described her anxiety and her difficulty in performing everyday tasks, the doctors tried her on all the various drugs: librium, saroten, valium, lergigan, nozinan, malorol, sordinol, haldol…

Ingeborg, who in the 1930s and 1940s had been known as the ward's little helper, who had enjoyed taking charge of the other patients in the kitchen, ended up in long-term geriatric care in Alingsås, with sores all over her body, constantly in tears, and *raising the roof* with her screams for help.

Her medical chart from September 15, 1978, shows that her neck was so severely bent back that she could not swallow when spoon-fed. The food had to be removed from her throat by suction. The likely cause of the contracture was tardive dyskinesia, a neurological condition induced by prolonged treatment with high doses of neuroleptic drugs. Two days later, Ingeborg passed away at the age of seventy-seven. I was thirteen and had just started high school.

Acknowledgments

This book would not have been possible without my aunt Ulla-Britt Andersson, Ingeborg's niece, who provided me with all the details I needed to begin searching public archives and medical records to reconstruct Ingeborg's life. Ulla-Britt also accompanied me for moral support on countless study visits.

Secondly, I should like to thank Jan Johansson, Ingeborg's great-nephew and my second cousin, for patiently guiding me through all the various branches of the family and figuring out who is who on hundreds of old black-and-white photographs. Jan was very generous with his time and knowledge of Vesene and the surrounding area, and provided me with valuable information by sharing everything from serious reference books, newspaper articles and interviews to tall tales and gossip. He also gave me some of Ingeborg's few surviving personal possessions, including an invitation to the children's funeral.

After two years studying academic dissertations, history books, local calendars, church records, maps, railway timetables, crime statistics and annual reports, I made contact with Artur's nieces Kerstin Lindström and Inga Andersson and his nephew Göte Davidsson. They kindly gave me photographs of the children when they were alive. Together with Lars Bertilsson, the verger of Vesene parish church, they provided invaluable assistance in returning the children's gravestone to public display in May 2016. I am deeply grateful to Göte for sharing his memories of the children's funeral, and for entrusting me with the letters that Ingeborg wrote to Artur from prison, which form the framework of my story.

My thanks to Carina and Johan Askengren for opening their home to a complete stranger and showing me the place where the tragedy occurred.

My thanks to Inga-Britt Blomdahl, Ingeborg's niece, for the loan of Ingeborg's postcard collection and photo album; to Ingeborg's other niece, my mother Astrid Rydnell, for preserving Ingeborg's rugs for posterity; and to Ingeborg's nephew, my uncle Göran Andersson, for sharing his memories of growing up with Ingeborg around.

My thanks to Ing-Gun Markegård for helping me make sense of old handwritten records; and to Peter du Rietz and Matilda Ljungqvist for tracking down articles in the newspaper archives in Gothenburg.

My thanks to Anita Andersson for the guided tour of Restad Hospital, Vänersborg; and to Barbro Bengtsson for the guided tour of Gäsene Courthouse, Ljung.

My thanks to Katarina Kallings and Ingrid Miljand at the Prison Museum of Sweden, Gävle; to Johanna Hästö at the Mental Health Museum, Säter; and to Christina Engström at the Swedish Railway Museum, Gävle.

My thanks to Magnus Gedda for talking to me about his grandfather, Pastor Dahlborg, and for showing me excerpts from the pastor's diaries.

My thanks to Britt-Inger Svahn for introducing me to relatives I didn't know I had, and for initiating me into the world of online genealogy.

My thanks to Stefan Ingesson and Anneli Petersson at the Regional State Archives, Vadstena; to Karin Ajaxon, Per Forsberg, Helena Liljekvist Sandblom and Tilde Lund at the Regional State Archives, Gothenburg; to Markus Maijala at the Swedish National Archives, Marieberg; to Jenny Spjuth Larsson at the Regional Archives, Vänersborg; to Anna Svensson at the Regional Archives, Gothenburg; and to Margareta Lundgren at Norra Älvsborg County Hospital, Trollhättan.

My thanks to Lena Almgren at the National Library of Sweden, Stockholm; to Eva-Lena Liljedahl at Herrljunga public library; to Dan Waldetoft at Nordiska Muséet, Stockholm; and to Thomas Lissing, freelance journalist, Växjö.

Many thanks to my brother Gunnar and my sister-in-law Tina Rydnell; to my cousin Marie-Louise Andersson; to my uncle Arne Andersson; and to my friends Svante Ljungqvist, Kirsi Oksman Ljungqvist, Sofia and Jesper Martell, Anna Pontén, Kristina W. Smith, Annika Söderlund, and Maria and Pelle Öhrn, for helping me obtain information, for letting me borrow their cars and driving me around, or for giving me a bed for the night in the course of my travels around Sweden in Ingeborg's footsteps.

Many thanks to my childhood friend Per Anders Wiktorsson, associate professor at Stockholm University; to assistant professors Ulrika Lif and Lotte Mjöberg and my fellow creative writing students at Mid Sweden University; to Sofia Ymén, my editor; and to my friends Christian Grønlund and Catharina Wrååk, for their valuable comments on the synopsis and the manuscript as a work in progress.

Finally, I should like to thank my publisher Stephanie Andén at Saga Egmont and all the residents of Vesene, old and new alike, for their interest, support and trust over the past three years. Over innumerable cups of coffee, savoury cakes and oat cookies, we shared fragmented memories and attempted to piece together the jigsaw puzzle that was Ingeborg's life.

Washington, DC, September 2018

Endnotes

1 English translation by John Christian Jacobi (1722) of the original German hymn *Ach Gott und Herr* by Martin Rutilius (1604), on which the Swedish hymn *Min synd, o Gud* sung at the funeral was also based.
   Source: Hymnary.org, https://hymnary.org/text/o_god_my_lord_how_greats_my_hoard
2 English translation by A.W. Almqvist (1884), now in public domain.
   Source: Project Gutenberg, http://www.gutenberg.org/files/20135/20135-h/20135-h.htm
3 English translation by John Kelly, believed to be of the same German hymn by Paul Gerhardt (1607–76) as that on which the Swedish hymn *Vänder om, I sorgse sinnen* (No. 389 in the 1819 hymn book used by Ingeborg) was based. Published in *Paul Gerhardt's Spiritual Songs*, London, 1867.
   Source: Project Gutenberg, http://www.gutenberg.org/files/30362/30362-h/30362-h.htm#c8

4 English translation (anonymous) of the original German hymn *Schönster Herr Jesu*, from which the Swedish hymn *Härlig är jorden* was also derived.
Source: Hymnary.org, https://hymnary.org/text/fairest_lord_jesus_ruler_of_all_nature